THOUGHT CATALOG BOOKS

# Hulk vs. Gawker

# Hulk vs. Gawker

THOUGHT CATALOG

Thought Catalog Books

Brooklyn, NY

# Contents

# Case Summary

Wrestling superstar Hulk Hogan was born Terry Gene Bollea in Georgia in 1953. He is possibly the most famous pro wrestler in world history.

Gawker Media is a constellation of websites whose flagship is Gawker.com, which focuses mainly on celebrity gossip.

In July 2007 while he was undergoing a divorce, Hogan had sex with Heather Clem, wife of his friend Todd Alan Clem, AKA shock radio host Bubba the Love Sponge. A bedroom surveillance camera filmed the encounter and two other sexual encounters between Hogan and Ms. Clem.

In October 2012, Gawker.com posted a 1:41 video excerpt from a half-hour reel of Hogan and Clem having sex. Hogan filed lawsuits against Gawker both for copyright infringement and invasion of privacy. The copyright infringement suit was quickly dismissed.

The main dramatic tension in the pretrial motions pits free speech rights versus privacy rights.

Hogan's lawyers argued that the only issue at hand was privacy. Not only did Hogan have no knowledge he was being recorded, there was also no newsworthiness in publishing a tape of Hogan having sex. Alleged racial comments he made on other tape reels—which Gawker had never seen and which were not the focus of the lawsuit—were therefore irrelevant and would only prejudice a jury against Hogan.

Gawker's lawyers argued that the reason Hogan filed a lawsuit against them was not because he was worried about the tape's sexual elements, but about the possibility of racial comments he'd allegedly made in other tapes being leaked to the public. They argued he feared that public knowledge of these comments would destroy his career just as similar comments had recently brought down public figures such as Paula Deen and Donald Sterling.

The landmark case is widely viewed as one of the most significant First Amendment trials in the new millennium. It could have huge and lasting effects on the future of digital media.

The highlights contained in this book are reprinted verbatim from court filings and documents in the public record. These selections have been edited for readability and clarity.

# 1

# Timeline

**July, 2007**...Hulk Hogan and Heather Clem have sex in Clem's bedroom while a surveillance camera films the encounter.

**March, 2012**...Reports of a Hulk Hogan sex tape surface in the media.

**September, 2012**...New York talent agent Tony Burton emails A. J. Daulerio of Gawker about whether he's interested in a Hulk Hogan sex video.

**October 4, 2012**...On Gawker.com, A.J. Daulerio posts an article titled "Even for a Minute, Watching Hulk Hogan Have Sex in a Canopy Bed is Not Safe For Work but Watch it Anyway."

**October 15, 2012**...Hogan's lawyers file two invasion-of-privacy lawsuits in Florida—one against Bubba Clem, the other against Gawker.

**October 29, 2012**...Hogan reaches a settlement with Bubba Clem, who publicly apologizes to Hogan. A few days later, Clem publicly states, "I am now convinced that Hulk Hogan was unaware of the presence of the recording device in my bedroom."

**December 14, 2012**…An alleged "sex tape broker" meets in a motel room with Hogan and attorney David Houston expecting to receive part of a $300,000 payout for returning the original copies of the video. Instead, the broker finds himself targeted in an FBI sting for alleged extortion.

**December 20, 2012**…A Federal District Court denies a motion by Hogan's attorneys against Gawker for copyright infringement. The Florida invasion-of-privacy lawsuit against Gawker continues apace.

**April 24, 2013**…A court orders Gawker to remove the video from their site.

**April 24, 2013**…Gawker publishes an article titled, "A Judge Told Us to Take Down Our Hulk Hogan Sex Tape Post. We Won't."

**July 2015**…WWE fires Hogan for alleged racist comments on a separate videotape not involved in the Gawker lawsuit.

**March 18, 2016**…A Florida jury finds that Gawker invaded Hogan's privacy and awards him roughly $140 million.

# 2

# The Players

**Terry Gene Bollea**, AKA wrestling superstar Hulk Hogan

**Todd Alan Clem**, AKA radio host Bubba the Love Sponge

**Heather Clem,** AKA Heather Cole, Bubba's ex-wife and the woman in the sex tape with Hogan

**Nick Denton**, Gawker CEO

**A. J. Daulerio**, ex-Gawker Editor-in-Chief who published a video clip and commentary on the Hogan sex tape

**Honorable James R. Case**, Florida judge presiding over certain pre-trial motions

**Seth Berlin**, Gawker Attorney

**Charles Harder**, Hulk Hogan's Attorney

# 3
—

# Hogan's Lawyers Make Their Case

**Highlights from legal motions by Hulk Hogan's lawyers:**

On October 4, 2012, Gawker posted on its flagship website, Gawker.com, a secretly recorded, explicit, pornographic video depicting the plaintiff, Terry Bollea (professionally known as Hulk Hogan), engaged in a private sexual encounter in a private bedroom, and depicting Mr. Bollea fully naked, aroused, and engaged in multiple sexual positions, with no aspect of the video blocked, blurred, pixelated or otherwise obscured (the "Sex Video"). Gawker posted the Sex Video, and left it up on the Internet, knowing, and not caring, that Mr. Bollea was unaware that he was recorded in the private bedroom, and also had not consented to its distribution. On the contrary, he strenuously protested any publication whatsoever and put the world on notice of the illegal filming. Gawker admitted that this was footage the public was "not supposed to see." The Sex Video was viewed by more than seven million (7,000,000) Internet voyeurs, resulting in a massive, highly intrusive, and long-lasting invasion of Mr. Bollea's privacy.

The individual defendants, Nick Denton and A. J. Daulerio, were directly involved in the publication. In October 2012,

Daulerio was Editor-in-Chief of Gawker.com. He received a 30-minute recording of Mr. Bollea's private sexual encounter, supervised the production of a one minute and 41 second "highlight reel" (in his words), and published that Sex Video, along with graphic commentary that he personally wrote, on Gawker.com. Nick Denton, Gawker's founder and CEO, was aware of and approved the publication of the Sex Video, and set the policies and practices at Gawker that gave rise to its publication.

Shortly before the Gawker Defendants' publication of the Sex Video, every single member of the editorial staff at Gawker.com had received actual notice that Mr. Bollea had been secretly filmed and was seeking criminal and civil prosecution of everyone involved in the filming or distribution/publication of the sex tape. Also, within 24 hours of the Gawker Defendants' publication of the Sex Video, Mr. Bollea's counsel sent Gawker two written cease and desist communications. Gawker responded in writing that it would not remove the Sex Video, and left it up at its website for millions to view.

The Motion for Summary Judgment obfuscates a key distinction between Gawker's publication of the Sex Video itself, and its publication of Daulerio's graphic commentary relating to it:

Mr. Bollea's complaint initially alleged claims arising out of both, however, Mr. Bollea made clear in April 2014, and has done so consistently since that time, that he is no longer pursuing a claim based on Daulerio's "commentary." Mr. Bollea does not seek, as Gawker's motion contends, any liability relating to the commentary. Moreover, Mr. Bollea does not seek to prevent anyone (Gawker or anyone else) from commenting or discussing his relationship with Heather Clem or the existence of a sex video. Mr. Bollea seeks to hold Gawker accountable for its publication of the Sex Video itself—showing the graphic video of him naked, aroused, and having sexual intercourse. The video itself was not a matter of public concern; it was not necessary to report the story about the existence of a sex tape involving Mr. Bollea and Ms. Clem, and it was cruel, despicable, and a gross invasion of Mr. Bollea's privacy....

The actual video footage of Mr. Bollea naked, aroused, and having sex in multiple positions, filmed without his knowledge or consent, was not and is not a matter of "public concern." The recording was of a private sexual encounter in a private bedroom. There is zero evidence that Mr. Bollea knew about the recording at the time it was made, or that he consented to the making or distribution of the Sex Video. Just the opposite, he aggressively sought to stop its publication, both before and after Gawker posted the Sex Video. Gawker admitted it received all of his notices. The Gawker Defendants also admitted that they did not care if he was secretly filmed or protested its publication, before and after Gawker published it. Gawker also admitted that it believed the Sex Video was surreptitiously recorded based on the footage in the video itself....

Daulerio's "commentary" that accompanied the Sex Video gave a "play-by-play" account of the entire video of Mr. Bollea's private sexual activity, and made clear Gawker's point that publishing the Sex Video was not supposed to be seen by members of the public, but Gawker instructed them to "watch it anyway." By contrast, news is material that people are supposed to see.

Gawker's internal communications show its executives bragging about how the Sex Video, as well as a story containing paparazzi photos of Duchess Kate Middleton's bare breasts taken while with a telephoto lens, had driven record amounts of traffic to the Gawker website, with the clear implication that Gawker's revenues would go through the roof.

Gawker's revenues did in fact go through the roof—they doubled during the two years following the publication of the Sex Video....

Mr. Bollea does not deny that he has allowed the public to learn certain specific aspects of his private life. However, Mr. Bollea emphatically denies that, in doing so, he has somehow waived his right to prohibit the publication of a secret video of him, naked and engaged in private sexual activity, in a private bedroom. Under the Gawker Defendants' skewed version of privacy, any famous person who has ever spoken publicly about sex, nudity, or going to the bathroom is powerless to stop a "peeping tom" with a video camera, or a video website, from secretly recording and publishing private footage of the person naked, having sex, or going to the bathroom.

If anything, the Gawker Defendants' parade of sleazy gossip and innuendo, which they submit in support of their Motion for Summary Judgment, proves precisely the opposite of their point: all those media outlets that covered Mr. Bollea's sex life, including even the *National Enquirer*, at least had the decency not to broadcast the Sex Video or any part of it. ...

The Gawker Defendants' argument is analogous to arguments made about rape victims that they supposedly forfeit their right to refuse consent to intercourse because they dress or act "sexy." Both arguments improperly conflate two different issues of consent, and argue that consent for one thing (dressing or acting sexy, in the case of a rape victim; or discussing nudity, sex, or going to the bathroom, in the case of an interview of a public figure) is consent for everything (rape; or publication of secretly-filmed private footage). That is not the law, and it could mean a wholesale end to privacy, and rape laws, if it were to become the law. ...

It speaks volumes that every other news outlet rejected the Gawker Defendants' judgment and reported the story of the Sex Video, without publishing the footage of nudity or sex....

The Gawker Defendants' electronic intrusion gave seven million people a front row seat in the bedroom to watch Mr. Bollea fully naked and having sex. That electronic intrusion of seclusion is just as actionable as if the intrusion were physical....

The evidence supports a jury finding that the Gawker Defendants' use of Mr. Bollea's likeness was "commercial" in nature based on, among other things, their expressed desire and clear efforts to use the Sex Video to drive maximum traffic to Gawker.com, and receive substantial financial benefits as a result, as well as the fact that Gawker succeeded in that dedl and doubled its traffic and revenues shortly after its publication of the Sex Video....

The Gawker Defendants' conduct in this lawsuit also is a warning shot to anyone who might consider attempting to prevent his or her private sexual activity from being broadcast to the world. The Gawker Defendants' position is that the decision to violate anyone's privacy is left solely up to them, and pursuant to their aggressive litigation tactics, anyone who seeks to enforce their privacy rights will have their entire private life "put on trial" by Gawker as punishment. If summary judgment is granted here, Americans will have only so much privacy as the CEO of Gawker decides to give us. When Gawker's CEO, Nick Denton, was asked whether Gawker sets "a lower value on privacy than most people do," he responded, "I don't think people give a f*ck, actually." …

Gawker Media, LLC, the company founded and run by Defendant Nick Denton, operates eight websites focusing on different interest areas ranging from sports to cars to women's issues. Gawker.com is its flagship website, described by a Gawker editor as a "tabloid at heart," and, according to Nick Denton, a website that adheres to the tagline: "without access, favor or discretion." … The writing style is admittedly "sexual" and "mean." … The subjects it covers, according to former Managing Editor, Emma Carmichael, amount to "yellow journalism" and, according to Master Lecturer of Journalism at the University of Florida, Professor Mike Foley, constitute "pornography."

Professor Foley explains in his expert report that journalists are ethically bound to "minimize harm" to the subjects about whom they report. … Gawker, however, does not believe in journalism ethics. Its stories pay no regard to whether they will cause harm.

Gawker's total disregard for ethical journalism originates from the top, namely, its CEO and founder, Defendant Nick Denton. The *Washington Post* quoted Denton as saying: "We don't seek to do good. We may inadvertently do good. We may inadvertently commit journalism. That is not the institutional intention."

Denton further described his philosophy at his deposition:

"I believe in total freedom and information transparency. I want everybody to know everything. And I think society, this country that I moved to will be better off if we could talk freely about everything. So that's ... I'm an extremist when it comes to that."

"The whole point of the company is that we trust our reporters to be smart and judicious without having to adopt the ethical pretense that what they're doing is anything but a sort of professionalized rudeness." —*Tommy Craggs, Executive Director of Deadspin, Gawker's sports website*

"Journalism ethics is nothing more than a measure of the scurrilousness your brand will bear." —*Tommy Craggs*

"Journalism ethics are the same as plumber ethics." —*John Cook, former Editor-in-Chief of Gawker.com, current Executive Editor for Investigations at Gawker Media*

A. J. Daulerio once posted an explicit video of a young and extremely intoxicated girl being sexually assaulted on the floor of a men's bathroom in a bar in Indiana, lying in a pool of urine. ... Daulerio admitted that the young girl may have been raped based on her high level of intoxication... When the girl and her father pleaded with Daulerio and Gawker's legal team to remove the video, Gawker responded: "This is a news story, and completely newsworthy. It's the truth, which can be hurtful, granted, but one's actions can have unintended consequences...we believe that we are publishing this legitimately and as such, we will not remove the clip." ...

If it were up to the Gawker Defendants, there would be no

privacy in America—everyone's secrets would be exposed, the intimate details of their lives would be fully published—and everyone would gather at Gawker to mock, ridicule, and gawk at what previously was confined to private conversations and closed bedroom doors. In other words, if it were up to Gawker, all walls would become windows, and no privacy would exist anywhere. David Carr, who covered media for *The New York Times*, analogized Gawker to a group of junior high school girls: "There was a group of ninth grade girls who knew everything, who saw everything, who said everything, the mean girls who just you know ran the show and laid waste to everyone they saw. That's Gawker. They rule the playground." ... Gawker's efforts to lay waste to everyone in their path is not journalism; it is, as Mr. Carr put it, "disgusting" and "despicable." ...

According to Denton, sex brings traffic, or, as he puts it: "Scandal sells....The staples of old yellow journalism are the staples of new yellow journalism: sex, crime; and, even better, sex crime." ... These are the kind of stories that Denton says cause advertisers to "shower [Gawker] with dollars" because they draw in unique viewers. ...

Gawker's disdain for journalism ethics, coupled with its insatiable appetite for traffic, revenues and profits is the reason we are here today. It is that sinister combination that makes Gawker unique among news organizations—no other news outlet aired any nudity or sexual content from the secretly-filmed, illegal recording of Mr. Bollea. ...

The testimony of Bubba Clem, Heather Clem and Terry Bollea is consistent on this point.

All three testified that the sexual encounter between Mr.

Bollea and Ms. Clem was not Mr. Bollea's idea. … Rather, Mr. Bollea was at a very low point in his life; he was physically, emotionally and legally separated from his wife, who made clear their marriage was permanently over and who had gone to live somewhere else. … When Mr. Bollea was at his most vulnerable, in mid-2007, the Clems lured Mr. Bollea into a sexual encounter with Heather in their private bedroom…and caused him to be filmed without his knowledge. … Bubba Clem later downloaded the secretly recorded footage onto a disc and took it to his office at the radio station. …

Every percipient witness with knowledge in this case has consistently testified that Mr. Bollea did not know that he had been filmed, did not know of the existence of a video of the encounter, and did not authorize the release or distribution of any such video. …

In March and April of 2012, rumors of a possible "Hulk Hogan sex tape" surfaced. … Mr. Bollea wanted it known, and told the press in no uncertain terms, that any such footage was secretly recorded illegally, that he knew nothing about it, never authorized it, and wanted the video never to "see the light of day."

Gawker itself was aware of Mr. Bollea's statements, because every member of the editorial staff at Gawker.com received the following press reports from emails to the Gawker Tips account on: March 7, 2012 ("Hulk Hogan says the sex tape being shopped to porn companies was 'secretly filmed' WITHOUT his permission…and claims the footage is nothing less than an 'outrageous invasion of privacy.' … Hulk's lawyer David Houston has released a statement … saying … 'We will take all necessary steps to enforce both civil and criminal liability.'"); March 8, 2012 ("The former WWE star says he was taped, and the video is being distributed, without his knowledge of the taping or permission to distribute it"); March 8, 2012 ("[Hulk] was adamant that he had no idea he was being taped and he would go after the people behind the tape both civilly and criminally ... Hulk and his lawyer could not have been clearer on TMZ Live yesterday...they don't want that tape to see the light of day"); March 12, 2012 ("Hogan says [the] tape was made without his knowledge"); and April 26, 2012 ("Hulk Hogan is freaking OUT over screen grabs of his alleged sex tape that have leaked onto the Internet"). ... Gawker's Managing Editor in March/April 2012, Emma Carmichael, confirmed that every member of Gawker's editorial staff, including all editors and all writers, received these Gawker Tips emails. ...

In late September 2012, A. J. Daulerio was approached via email by talent agent Tony Burton of Buchwald & Associates in New York about whether he was interested in a video of "Hulk Hogan" having sex. ... Notwithstanding Gawker's actual awareness that the video had been illegally recorded, illegally obtained, illegally shopped to third parties, and Mr. Bollea and his attorney were aggressively pursuing both criminal and civil remedies against everyone involved—Defendant Daulerio expressed immediate interest in the video.

The video arrived in the mail from an anonymous source. Once the video arrived at Gawker's offices, Gawker employees immediately started watching it and commenting on it. ... Gawker produced internal e-mails and instant messages of its employees making fun of Mr. Bollea, including his genitals, and making cruel comments about the Sex Video. ... The inter-office commentary undermines Gawker's contention that its purpose in publishing the video was to inform the public and report "the news." The matter was an office joke to Gawker, with no consideration to the people whose lives hung in the balance.

Gawker.com's Managing Editor at the time, Emma Carmichael, testified that she was the first person to watch the video at Gawker:

"Q. Was it assumed at Gawker that [Terry Bollea] did not approve the release of the sex video?
A. Yes.
Q. The camera was from a very high point of view, correct?
A. Yes.
Q. And the camera appeared to be fairly far away from the bed, correct?
A. As best as I could recall, yes.
Q. Of the video that you saw, did you ever see Hulk Hogan or the female look into the camera?
A. From what I saw, no, they did not."

The video contains no indication that Mr. Bollea was aware of a camera present. Editor-in-Chief A.J. Daulerio admitted this during his deposition:

"Q. ....Have you ever seen any evidence that Hulk Hogan knew at the time of the encounter that that encounter was being videotaped?
A. No."

The video was shot from an angle above and far away from the bed, as if from a camera at or near the ceiling, and the footage appeared to be from a surveillance camera.

But those facts made no difference to Gawker's editorial decision-making. A .J. Daulerio testified that he saw no difference between someone being surreptitiously recorded and someone who voluntarily recorded himself having sex, and further testified that he would have published the Sex Video even if he knew definitively that it was surreptitiously recorded without Mr. Bollea's consent....

Despite knowing the illegal circumstances under which the footage was recorded and distributed, and despite the mysterious circumstances surrounding the anonymous receipt of the video:

No one at Gawker contacted Terry Bollea, or his lawyer, David Houston, or Heather or Bubba Clem...presumably because Gawker knew they would not give permission to publish ... and ...

No one at Gawker blocked, blurred or pixelated Mr. Bollea's and Heather Clem's private parts or sexual acts before broadcasting them to the world...even though Gawker admits it had the ability to do so ... The Gawker Defendants instead edited the video to include footage of each of Mr. Bollea's and Heather Clem's multiple sexual positions, sexual acts, their oral sex, and Mr. Bollea aroused.

Gawker editors A. J. Daulerio and Emma Carmichael expressly instructed video editor Kate Bennert to include explicit footage of Mr. Bollea having sex, and to include footage of Mr. Bollea aroused. ... Gawker did not, as it argues, show "only enough" of the sex tape to prove to the audience that the tape existed, and included sex. A pixelated still, or a pixelated one or two seconds of footage, would have accomplished that goal, if Gawker had such a goal. On the contrary, Gawker created a "highlight reel"—the very term used by Editor-in-Chief A. J. Daulerio to describe the video that he and his staff produced and broadcast to the world. ...

On October 4, 2012, Gawker did what no other news outlet or website had done, although several outlets reported on the alleged contents of the video: Gawker published the Sex Video.

Journalism Professor Mike Foley, a Master Lecturer at the University of Florida and a former award-winning reporter, editor, and senior executive at the *St. Petersburg Times* (now the *Tampa Bay Times*), states in his affidavit, based on his 40 years of journalistic experience, that:

(1) While the story that Mr. Bollea had sex with Heather Clem and that a sex tape existed was news, the publication of the actual content of the Sex Video was not newsworthy—rather, it was "pornography." ...

(2) Journalists routinely avoid publishing material that is invasive of people's privacy unless absolutely necessary to tell the story. ...

(3) Where such material is necessary to the story, journalists use the least invasive material available. ...

(4) Specifically, where stories involve video footage of persons in the nude in private settings (such as stories of women who were secretly recorded in locker rooms), journalistic outlets never run the footage. ...

(5) It was not necessary for Gawker to publish the Sex Video to tell the story of its existence and the circumstances surrounding it. ...

Further, former Editor-in-Chief of Gawker.com, Defendant Daulerio himself admitted under oath that the inclusion of footage of Mr. Bollea's penis was not newsworthy. Instead, it was included merely to "add color" to Mr. Daulerio's "commentary."

The so-called "commentary"—entitled "Even for a Minute, Watching Hulk Hogan Have Sex in a Canopy Bed is Not Safe For Work But Watch it Anyway"—reads like lurid voyeurism, not news. It includes: (1) a headline that directs readers to watch the Sex Video; (2) an admission that when readers watch famous people have sex, they are "shameless voyeurs and deviants;" (3) an admission that "we are not supposed to see" the Sex Video; (4) a graphic description of the sex acts and positions of Mr. Bollea and Ms. Clem; (5) a graphic description of Mr. Bollea aroused; (6) a graphic description of the noises made by Mr. Bollea at the point of climax; (8) and an admission that the Sex Video contains "not safe for work" content (a common Internet description of pornographic content). ... None of these descriptions of Mr. Bollea constitute a matter of public concern. The private nature of the acts (nudity and sex), the private location (a private bedroom), the secret filming of Mr. Bollea, and the admission by Gawker and

Daulerio that it is something we are "not supposed to see" is overwhelming evidence of the private nature of the Sex Video, and therefore not a matter of "public concern." Likewise, the commentary is not, as Gawker contends, commentary on Mr. Bollea's public image, or his relationship with Ms. Clem, or his relationship with his ex-wife Linda, or his sex life generally, or for that matter commentary on any of the interviews or press coverage of Mr. Bollea, copies of which were attached to Defendants' Motion for Summary Judgment. Rather, the commentary is simply gratuitous descriptions of sex and admissions that it is something that people are "not supposed to see"—as opposed to news, which is something that people are supposed to see....

Mr. Bollea swiftly reacted to the publication of the Sex Video. His counsel wrote Gawker, stating that the video was surreptitiously recorded, released without his consent, and that the continued publication of it was offensive and harmful to Mr. Bollea, and demanded its removal. ... Gawker refused to take the Sex Video down, and Defendant Denton (founder and CEO) called Mr. Bollea's pleas to his humanity "not persuasive."

After filing this lawsuit, Mr. Bollea moved for a temporary injunction from this Court, and the Court entered an order enjoining the publication of the Sex Video and the accompanying "commentary." Gawker refused to comply with the Court's order. Instead, Gawker published a story entitled "A Judge Told Us to Take Down Our Hulk Hogan Post. We Won't." ... As the headline promised, Gawker refused to remove the commentary in violation of the court order, and though it did remove the Sex Video from Gawker.com, it simultaneously added a link to the same Gawker-edited Sex Video at a third party site, directing viewers to continue to watch the court-enjoined Sex Video. ... Although the temporary injunction order eventually was reversed, Gawker never even pretended to obey it when it was in force, choosing instead to continue to violate Mr. Bollea's privacy.

Perhaps even more egregious, during the course of this litigation, the Gawker Defendants threatened through their counsel to publish additional footage of Mr. Bollea having sexual intercourse. ... Emma Carmichael also testified at her deposition that a second sex video of Mr. Bollea was edited and produced by Gawker, but has not yet been published to Gawker.com. ... The Gawker Defendants' threat hangs like the Sword of Damocles over Mr. Bollea, as he continues to seek to protect his privacy and seek appropriate remedies for the Gawker Defendants' 2012...2013 violation of his privacy. ...

From October 4, 2012 through April 25, 2013, at least 5.35 million unique visitors flocked to the Gawker.com webpage. ... At least 2.5 million people watched the Sex Video at Gawker.com ... and an additional 4.5 million people watched the same Gawker-produced Sex Video at other websites (mostly porn sites) that had lifted the video from Gawker.com, for a total of at least 7 million total views. ... The Sex Video generated the second-most page views of any Gawker.com story in 2012, and spiked Google searches for the term "Gawker" (not Hulk or Hogan sex tape) to their highest level throughout the history of Gawker.com, both past and present. ...

Gawker used the Sex Video as a form of advertisement

for Gawker—a way to bring users into the Gawker universe where they could then become available to Gawker's advertisers and generate revenue and profits for Gawker. ... The Gawker Defendants' sex tape expert, Kevin Blatt, testified that advertising revenue is generated by publishing a celebrity sex tape on a website, even if the celebrity sex tape is posted for free. ... Blatt himself has used a celebrity sex tape to promote traffic to a website, much like the Gawker Defendants did here. ...

According to Gawker's corporate designee, COO Scott Kidder, Gawker had an employee bonus program tied to traffic and paid the maximum possible employee bonus to Gawker employees during the month of October 2012 because of the traffic generated by the Sex Video. ... Denton and Daulerio admitted that, if the story had been published without the Sex Video, it would have generated significantly less traffic. ...

Denton bragged that the publication of the Sex Video, along with Gawker's earlier publication of the surreptitiously-taken photos of Duchess Kate Middleton's breasts, boosted daily U.S. traffic to Gawker.com to over one million users per day for the first time ever (stating Gawker "scored with royal breasts and Hulk sex" and boasting about the huge traffic those stories brought to Gawker.com). ...

Mr. Bollea suffered a breakdown as a result of the publication of the Sex Video. He testified that it destroyed his life. He could not function, sleep, eat, or think straight. ... Gawker's release of the Sex Video was the most stressful situation Mr. Bollea ever faced in his life. ... Mr. Bollea has cried, worried about its impact on his children, and its impact on his current marriage, and he often is confronted by strangers in public who have seen the Sex Video and try to engage him in conversation about it, often with his wife and/or children present. ...

Gawker argues that, as a matter of law, the Sex Video is a matter of public concern. In making this argument, Gawker misstates the law and conflates reporting about Mr. Bollea's sex life with publishing actual footage of Mr. Bollea fully naked and having sex. ...

The Gawker Defendants' motion does not address any of the following numerous facts, which create triable issues as to whether the Sex Video is and was a matter of legitimate public concern:

(1) The fact that video footage of Mr. Bollea fully naked and engaged in explicit sexual acts was not necessary to report the story of Mr. Bollea's relationship with Ms. Clem or the existence of a sex tape from their encounter.

(2) The fact that the pornography in the Sex Video is a result of a deliberate editorial decision of Gawker to include that explicit material and make a "highlight reel" of it.

(3) The fact that the explicit content of the Sex Video was marketed to the public as pornography ("not safe for work"), and thus is not journalism.

(4) The fact that the Gawker Defendants had the technical ability to block, blur, or pixelate the footage, which would allow them to report on the existence of the Sex Video, while protecting Mr. Bollea's privacy.

(5) The fact that numerous news outlets reported the same

"story" as the Gawker Defendants—of the existence of the sex tape and Mr. Bollea's relationship with Bubba and Heather Clem—but correctly did so without publishing any sexually explicit footage.

(6) The fact that Gawker's executives, including CEO Nick Denton, have been publicly disdainful of privacy rights in general.

(7) The fact that Gawker's business is to routinely publish explicit sexual content, such as the Sex Video, to generate traffic and readership, and thereby generate revenues and profits.

(8) The fact that the Gawker Defendants' publication of the Sex Video is a violation of established standards of journalism ethics, which Gawker's management says that it does not believe in anyway.

(9) The fact that the Gawker Defendants' publication of the Sex Video is consistent with a longstanding course of conduct whereby Gawker has repeatedly and routinely invaded people's privacy for no journalistic reason at all, including the incidents involving ESPN reporter Erin Andrews, Duchess Kate Middleton, actress Rebecca Gayheart, and NFL quarterback Brett Favre, as well as publication of footage of the young woman in Indiana being sexually assaulted in the bathroom of a sports bar. As confirmed by the testimony of University of Florida Journalism Professor Mike Foley, who served for 40 years at the *St. Petersburg Times*, Gawker has consistently acted as pornographers, not journalists.

The fact that Gawker.com's then-Editor in Chief A. J.

Daulerio admitted that it was not necessary to show Mr. Bollea's penis in the Sex Video to report the news, and then-Managing Director Emma Carmichael admitted it was not necessary to link to the nude video of Erin Andrews to tell the story of her peeping tom, but Gawker did both anyway. ...

First, the Gawker Defendants broadcast forty-five seconds, not nine, of Mr. Bollea naked. That footage is just as invasive of Mr. Bollea's privacy as the footage of him having sex. Second, 100% of the one minute and 41 second Sex Video consisted of pre-sex dialogue, sex, and post-sex dialogue, all of which is highly invasive and highly embarrassing. Third, even assuming the absurd premise that only the nine seconds "counts," the Gawker Defendants do not gain the right to invade Mr. Bollea's privacy and publish explicit footage of Mr. Bollea naked and having sex simply because they also published a greater amount of footage that supposedly was "less invasive," and less explicit. ...

Upon receipt of the 30-minute video of Mr. Bollea, Gawker employees immediately watched the video and made cruel comments about the video and Mr. Bollea in internal e-mails and messages.

Approximately 4.5 million people watched the Gawker-produced video at other websites that had lifted the video from Gawker.com. ...

(...)

Who stole the sex tape from Bubba Clem and sent it to Gawker? The issue is irrelevant, and already has been determined through document discovery. It is undisputed that Gawker obtained a 30 minute sex tape from Tony Burton of the Buchwald Agency in New York; edited the footage into a 1 minute and 41 second "highlight reel" (the term used by Gawker's own editor-in-chief A. J. Daulerio); and published it for six consecutive months at Gawker.com, where millions of people watched it. Documents produced by Burton and the Buchwald Agency show that Mike "Cowhead" Calta (Bubba Clem's on-air competitor) was involved in sending the 30-minute tape to his agent Burton, who then sent the tape to A.J. Daulerio of Gawker. ...

Importantly, this case is about Gawker's acts that violated Mr. Bollea's privacy rights and caused him substantial damages. Yet at every turn, Gawker has sought to use this litigation as a means to repeatedly punish Mr. Bollea for bringing this case, seeking to violate his personal, financial and sexual privacy, and seeking to interfere with his personal and business relationships, cause harm to his career, harass him with numerous sets of written discovery, multiple long days of a videotaped deposition, repeated meritless motions seeking terminating sanctions, endless nonparty discovery and depositions, at a substantial cost, both economic and psychological. All this, together, amounts to continued injustice by Gawker against Mr. Bollea. The end result is justice turned on its head—where a plaintiff, wronged by a defendant, is forced to undergo a process that is so long in duration (well over 2 years), so expensive, so inconvenient, harassing and oppressive, and so threatening to the plaintiff's career, that seeking and obtaining justice becomes a virtual impossibility.

(...)

Gawker also falsely contends that one of the redacted terms is included in a "pivotal comment" in the case....The "comment" Gawker refers to is where Bubba Clem allegedly says, "if we ever did want to retire, all we have to do is use that…footage of him…."

To call the alleged quote "pivotal" is misleading and preposterous. Neither Mr. Bollea's privacy invasion claim, nor Gawker's "newsworthiness" and "public concern" defenses, rest in any way on Mr. Clem's alleged comment on an alleged video that Gawker never possessed or published.

Gawker readily admits that its business is to publish private, salacious material. See, e.g., Exhibit A (Deposition Exhibit 36; in which Nick Denton, CEO of Gawker, sent an email to his staff regarding "traffic" to Gawker.com, stating: "We scored with royal breasts [referring to its publication of Duchess Kate Middleton sunbathing topless at a private residence] and (this month) Hulk sex."). Thus, the fact that Gawker's business is to make money by publishing embarrassing and damaging information about celebrities is hardly a "canard," as Gawker contends…but rather is a fact.

(…)

Gawker makes much of a letter from an Assistant U.S. Attorney that lists three videos, two of which are dated the same day (thus, they could be copies of the same video) and a third that has no date (and could be a third copy of the same video). …

Gawker asks that it be allowed to call Plaintiff a racist in front of the jury, based on [information] by an unknown person and sent by an extortionist, of an alleged video that no one in this case has ever seen, and that is irrelevant to this case because any such video was not posted by Gawker. …

The documents created by an unknown extortionist purporting that there might possibly be as many as three different videos, are unauthenticated, lack foundation, are unreliable, and are hearsay. No party in this action is aware of any more than one video, and the only identifiable witness with actual knowledge is Bubba Clem, who solely created the video testified under oath that, to his knowledge, there exists only one sex video, and not more. ...

Instead, the only specific evidentiary sanction that Gawker requests is a ridiculous one: that Gawker be permitted to introduce to the jury unauthenticated, irrelevant, highly prejudicial, hearsay evidence of alleged use of offensive language relating to race, without objection.

(...)

The issue the jury will decide is whether the video Gawker published online on its website showing images and audio of Mr. Bollea naked and engaged in sexual intercourse was a matter of legitimate public concern.

As part of a systematic defense strategy to defend this case by attacking Mr. Bollea personally, Gawker is persisting in efforts to obtain and use alleged additional video footage of Mr. Bollea and Heather Clem involving encounters other than the encounter at issue in this case.

This alleged additional video footage was the subject of an FBI investigation emanating from an attempt to extort Mr. Bollea using such alleged footage.

Bollea 002654-2667 consists of text messages between Mr. Bollea and Bubba Clem in which, among other things, Mr. Bollea refers to the media reports about the alleged recordings....Mr. Bollea did not and does not have personal knowledge whether there exist more recordings than the 30-minute video that was sent to regarding whether more than one tape exists. Mr. Clem stated at the time, and testified at his deposition, that he is aware of only one disk containing a recording, and that disk was stolen from him.

It is undisputed that Mr. Bollea was illegally recorded without his knowledge or consent. These alleged additional recordings do not refute these facts.

Rather, the only purpose evidence of these alleged additional recordings serves is to inflame and prejudice the jury against Mr. Bollea.

There is nothing within the documents produced during discovery demonstrating that these recordings contain any evidence that Mr. Bollea knew he was being recorded or consented to being recorded.

The alleged use of offensive language, even if it occurred, is not probative of any material fact underlying the claims and defenses at issue in this litigation. ...

Even if the alleged offensive language were somehow relevant, and its probative value is not substantially outweighed by prejudice, it is nothing more than rank hearsay of an extortionist, who was seeking money in exchange for delivery of the recordings....

Again, these statements are alleged summaries of alleged recordings, created by an unknown person as part of an extortion attempt; there is no evidence the recordings actually exist or contain the language included on the alleged summaries.

(...)

Plaintiff sought the assistance of the F.B.I. to investigate and prosecute an attempt to extort him with the secret footage of him naked and having sex. The alleged other video has never been a legitimate issue in this case, and Plaintiff certainly has never tried to make it an issue. Just the opposite: Gawker Defendants have repeatedly tried to make the alleged other video an issue for the purpose of further invading Plaintiff. Plaintiff has consistently opposed these efforts. Thus, the premise of the Gawker Defendants motion that Plaintiff filed this public lawsuit supposedly for the ulterior purpose of keeping the alleged other video private even at issue, and Plaintiff certainly has never tried to make it one defies logic, lacks support, and is false.

Gawker Defendants have publicly stated to the press in recent weeks that they are facing the prospect of being economically destroyed by a jury verdict. Gawker Defendants therefore are now resorting to jury nullification by seeking to brand Plaintiff as a racist to the jury and the general public. Such improper tactics have no place in jurisprudence which seeks justice above all else. Gawker Defendants seek to turn the court system on its head and use it as a means to destroy Plaintiff and deny him a fair trial on his legitimate claims.

It also is noteworthy that Gawker Defendants are not arguing that this evidence is relevant to establish Plaintiff [alleges knowledge] of being recorded, or any other potentially legitimate issue in the case. Rather, the motion is frivolous, and possibly even warrants sanctions given the patent absurdity of its central premise, as well as its total lack of factual support.

An extortionist (who will not testify at trial) prepared purported written summaries of alleged video to try to steal money from Plaintiff. Websites made unverified comments about its alleged existence and contents. None of the authors of these purported summaries or stories will testify at trial.

Gawker Defendants maintain that the relevancy of the video is based on the alleged use of offensive language. ...

Gawker Defendants cannot establish that the evidence is competent or relevant, let alone that it meets the heightened threshold required when a party attempts to admit evidence of highly offensive language of this type. Gawker motion should be denied in its entirety, and their attorneys and all of their witnesses should be specifically instructed that they must not raise any of these issues in their testimony or arguments at trial at any time.

(...)

Gawker Media, LLC ("Gawker") operates a group of celebrity tabloid websites that publish, among other things, salacious content that invades the privacy of celebrities. See, e.g., Fred Durst: Touch My Balls and My Ass and Then Sue Gawker, Gawker.com (printed Oct. 2, 2013) (after Fred Durst sues Gawker for invasion of privacy, Gawker writes: "Someone sent us a link to a video of your penis, we went into shock, and we shared it with the world for about 2 hours."); Max Read, Three Topless Photos of Kate Middleton Put Us at Two for Three on Royal Nudie Pic Scandals [NSFW] (Updated), Gawker.com (Sept. 14, 2012) (publishing the topless photos and stating, "isn't this the classy way to have your privacy invaded?"); A. J. Daulerio, Brett Favre's Cellphone Seduction of Jenn Sterger (Update), Deadspin.com (Oct. 7, 2010) (posting video obtained from "third party," which includes, in Daulerio's own words: "penis photos at the 2:08 mark"). ...

First, Gawker is in the business of publishing gossip that invades the privacy of celebrities. ... Thus, Gawker should not have access to information regarding the alleged private statements of Plaintiff that have nothing to do with the issues of this case, and have the potential to cause him harm.

Second, the redacted terms at issue are inadmissible hearsay—statements that allegedly appear in a video that neither Gawker nor Plaintiff has a copy of, and which has never been produced in discovery in this case. As such, there is no evidentiary foundation for the alleged statements.

Third, whether or not Plaintiff used offensive language in a video that Gawker did not post and thus has nothing to do with the claims in this action is simply not relevant to any of the claims or defenses in this case. Plaintiff is not suing Gawker for any reporting on purportedly offensive language—he is suing Gawker for publishing a voyeuristic video depicting him fully naked and engaged in explicit sexual activity and distributed without his knowledge or consent. The case has nothing to do with offensive language allegedly appearing in videos that are not at issue. Thus, discovery of such comments will not lead to evidence that will actually be admitted at trial.

(...)

To the best of [Hogan]'s recollection, there were at least two, and possibly three, sexual encounters with Heather Clem in her private bedroom at the Clems' residence, and one brief sexual encounter with Heather Clem at the radio station of Todd Clem's radio program. To the best of [Hogan]'s recollection, these encounters all occurred in approximately late spring/early summer of 2007, after [Hogan] had separated from his wife.

(...)

During a period of approximately two years before [Hogan]

had sexual relations with Heather Clem, Todd Clem urged [Hogan], on numerous occasions, to have sexual relations with Heather Clem. [Hogan] turned him down repeatedly throughout that time, and told Mr. Clem to stop bringing up the subject. In approximately late spring/early summer of 2007, after [Hogan] had separated from his wife, [Hogan] gave in to the urgings of Mr. Clem and Heather Clem, and discussed the issue with Mr. Clem at that time.

In or about Spring 2012, [Hogan] asked Mr. Clem to explain the media reports regarding allegations of a possible sex tape involving [Hogan]. Mr. Clem denied having any knowledge of or involvement in a sex tape. At no time prior to or during the sexual encounter with Ms. Clem did either Mr. or Ms. Clem ever state or imply to [Hogan] that the encounter would be recorded. If such a statement had been made, [Hogan] would not have consented to the recording, and would not have engaged in a recorded sexual encounter. At no time did [Hogan] know that he would or might be recorded, and at no time did he give consent to anyone to either record the encounter or to disseminate any portion of a recording of the encounter to anyone.

(...)

Bubba Clem gave extensive testimony that Ms. Clem both knew about the Secret Recording at the time it was made, and knew that Mr. Clem had burned a DVD copy of the Secret Recording (the copy which apparently was stolen and sent to Gawker).

Ms. Clem herself admitted that she knew Bubba Clem had burned a CD of the Secret Recording, because he showed it to her.

Terry Bollea testified that both Heather and Bubba Clem pressured and goaded him into having the sexual encounter with Heather, which gives rise to an inference that Heather knew that the sex would be recorded.

During the course of Mr. Bollea's friendship with Mr. Clem, both Bubba and Heather Clem pressured and goaded Mr. Bollea into having a sexual encounter with Ms. Clem. ... ("she started asking me to have sex with her on the phone") ... (there were at least 20 conversations; "they [the Clems] kept bringing it up"); ... ("Bubba made me think that Heather was initiating it") ... In 2007, after Mr. Bollea had separated from his now ex-wife Linda, and when he was at a low point in his life ... the Clems again asked him to have sex with Heather, and this time Mr. Bollea went along with it. ... ("After...the marriage was dysfunctional...and...I was under the understanding that my marriage was over. Q. [D]id you come to Bubba and ask if the offer still stood? A. No. Q. How did it come up again? A. Somehow or another, I was just really depressed....And I went over to his house, and Heather pursued me while I was there. And I just let my guard down."). Mr. Bollea and Ms. Clem thereafter engaged in sexual relations in a private bedroom in Ms. Clem's house.

Unbeknownst to Mr. Bollea, there was a surveillance camera located in the bedroom, disguised as a small motion detector, painted the same color as the wall, and placed high up where the wall meets the ceiling. ... Heather Clem was a resident of the house and knew its existence and placement. ... It is reasonable to infer that she knew her sexual encounter with Mr. Bollea was being recorded, and her responses to discovery confirm her knowledge and involvement.

Mr. Bollea was surreptitiously recorded, and did not know about the Secret Recording until almost five years later. A copy of the Secret Recording eventually was anonymously sent to Gawker, which edited and produced a one minute and 41 second "highlight reel" (in the words of Gawker.com's Editor in Chief, A. J. Daulerio, who produced the video with his staff) containing explicit footage of Mr. Bollea fully naked, aroused, and engaging in multiple positions of sexual intercourse.

# 4

# Gawker's Lawyers Respond

**Highlights from legal motions by Gawker's lawyers:**

In public and in this Court, plaintiff Terry Bollea, professionally known as Hulk Hogan, has alleged that this case is about the harm caused by a tape depicting him having sex. In private, however, Hogan admitted a very different motivation for filing suit: He wanted to protect his public image after being told that the sex tape(s) included footage of him making "several racial slurs."

In the Spring of 2012, a timeline of Hulk Hogan sex tapes circulated in the Tampa radio community. The timeline showed that during his filmed encounters with the Clems, Hogan used several racial slurs. A website then published still photos from a sex tape filmed in the Clems' bedroom and suggested that the tape showed Hogan making statements "about black people." After Gawker later posted the Video Excerpts, Hogan was told that a sex tape showed him making "several racial slurs." As the timetable of events makes clear, that knowledge is what prompted this lawsuit.

Indeed, shortly before he filed suit, Hogan sent a text message to his best friend, Bubba the Love Sponge Clem, making clear his motivation. As Hogan explained to Clem, "I have a PPV [pay-per-view] and I am not waiting for any more surprises because we know there is a lot more coming." Specifically, Hogan expressed to Clem his real concern: "[w]e know there's more than one tape out there" and "were told" that one "has several racial slurs."...

1. During discovery, the Special Discovery Magistrate ordered that each racial slur and reference to African Americans in the documents produced by plaintiff and third-party witnesses, as well as all deposition testimony referring to racial slurs and African Americans, be redacted. For this reason, the Publisher Defendants have included the term "[REDACTED]" in this motion and the accompanying exhibits wherever the actual text of the exhibits or testimony includes redacted racial slurs or references to African Americans. If requested, the unredacted documents and videotaped deposition testimony will be provided to the Court for in camera review.

2. In the following days, as the news of a Hogan sex tape spread, a timeline of two Hogan sex tapes circulated through the Tampa radio community. ... The timeline showed that Hogan made two racial slurs while talking with Bubba and Heather Clem, as well as a "real [REDACTED] comment." ... It also showed that at the end of one tape, Bubba Clem allegedly said to Heather that "[i]f we ever did want to retire all we have to do is use that footage of [Hogan] talking about [REDACTED] people."

3. Within weeks, a website called The Dirty posted two items that included still images from a Hogan sex tape. ... Along

with the images, the second posting included the following caption: "Terry, do you remember what you said about black people in this sex tape?"

4. On October 4, 2012, Gawker posted the Video Excerpts. Those excerpts contained only 101 seconds of footage from a tape that runs more than a half hour....

5. In the wake of Gawker's posting, Hogan went on a media tour to promote an upcoming wrestling pay-per-view event. During the tour, he talked about the sex tape and his sexual encounter with Heather Clem extensively to various national media. Although Hogan and his lawyer told reporters that they were going to initiate legal action, they did not.

(...)

9. On October 11, [attorney David] Houston and Davidson spoke by telephone. ... During that conversation, Davidson said that the first sex tape was sent to Gawker "to send a warning shot" to Hogan. ...Davidson told Houston that Hogan should "pay him because otherwise there would be increasing problems for Mr. Hogan." ...

In the text message, Hogan told Clem that "things are moving really fast" and expressed the reason for his concern:

"We know there's more than one tape out there and a [sic] one that has several racial slurs were [sic] told. I have a PPV [pay-per-view] and I am not waiting for anymore surprises because we know there is a lot more coming."

Two days later, on October 17, Howard Stern interviewed Bubba Clem about the sex tape and Hogan's lawsuit. During the interview, the two men had the following exchange:

HOWARD STERN: Let's say he really is embarrassed by this. Let's say everything that they are reporting, these rumors that the "N" word is being said ...
MR. CLEM: But he said it.

Hogan's text message is relevant to show his motivation for filing this lawsuit and to undercut his claim that he was harmed by the excerpts Gawker posted. It is undisputed that Hogan did not file suit or seek an injunction until after he learned that sex tape(s) depicted him making "several racial slurs." Indeed, the evidence shows that Hogan's concern was not being depicted engaged in sexual activity ... after all, he routinely talked about his sex life and body parts on national television and radio, and even discussed these supposedly "private" matters after Gawker's posting, even joking about them.

---

EVIDENCE THAT A PARTY MADE RACIAL SLURS IS ADMISSIBLE EVEN THOUGH IT MIGHT BE PREJUDICIAL.

As explained above, however, Hogan's text message referring to "several racial slurs" is not hearsay (it is a party admission)...

Here, the evidence of Hogan's racial slurs is plainly relevant. His text message to Bubba Clem about the tapes showing him using "several racial slurs" establishes his motivation for filing suit and undercuts his claim that he was harmed by the Gawker excerpts.

The Publisher Defendants have a good faith basis for seeking to admit this evidence. The fact that a Hogan sex tape included racial slurs was:

- Reported in the press before and after Gawker's posting,
- Included in a timeline of two tapes that was produced by a third-party witness and that was discussed among people in the Tampa radio community,
- Included in a transcript of a tape provided to Hogan's lawyer by a person seeking to establish the authenticity of the tapes and to show that they could cause "increasing problems for Mr. Hogan," and
- Is the subject of a text message sent by Hogan himself.

---

On October 15, 2012, later in that same thread of messages, Hogan texted the following to Mr. Clem: "Why are there 3 tapes out there"? ... That fact—that there are three sex tapes featuring Hogan and Mrs. Clem—has never been publicly reported. In addition, the media reports about the existence of additional sex tapes containing racial slurs were not published until after Hogan's October 12, 2012 text message. ... (Philly.com article, dated October 18, 2012, reporting that "[a] source says he saw footage on one of the surreptitious recordings of Hogan ... using the N-word and making other derogatory remarks about black people"); ... Again, a jury could look at this evidence, conclude that Hogan had at that point received credible information about the existence of an additional sex tape depicting him using racist language, and conclude from that and other associated conduct that that is what was actually aggrieving him when he filed the lawsuits.

Hogan is additionally incorrect in denigrating the potential probative value of what he calls "the 'summaries'" of the sex tape content (and what the Publisher Defendants have been calling the "timeline and transcript documents") by saying that they "were prepared by an extortionist trying to steal money from [Hogan] in exchange for an agreement not to release the alleged recordings." The timeline document, which was produced by a third party in response to Hogan's subpoena, was attached to an email dated March 12, 2012. ... Davidson, the supposed extortionist, did not enter the picture until October 10, 2012. ... And, the reason that Davidson provided the transcript document to Houston was to authenticate what was on the tapes he sought to sell to Hogan, knowing the videos would be watched to verify the transcripts....

It is true that, in April 2012, a website called The Dirty alluded to the possibility of racial slurs when it posted still images from a Hogan sex tape. ... ("Terry, do you remember what you said about black people in this sex tape?"). But, Hogan testified at his deposition that he did not see that post. ... And, prior to October 12, 2012, no publication had reported that there was other sex tapes involving Hogan and Heather Clem, in addition to the one Gawker had reported about, nor that any of those tapes contained footage of Hogan using racial slurs.

(...)

Even though Bollea's responses are not full and complete, it is now readily apparent why Bollea resisted production. The documents and limited supplemental interrogatory responses he provided demonstrate that, for close to a year, Bollea made material misrepresentations both in other sworn interrogatory responses and in sworn deposition testimony. They also demonstrate that, through his counsel, Bollea made material misrepresentations to both Judge Case and Judge Campbell about key facts, the status of the FBI investigation, and Bollea's compliance with earlier discovery rulings. And, they explain, at least in significant part, why Bollea and his counsel hid the FBI documents and related information ... namely, to avoid revealing that transcripts of a recording of Bollea having sexual relations with Heather Clem show that (a) Bollea used several racial epithets and made other racist comments during that encounter and (b) Bubba Clem's pivotal "we could retire off this tape" statement referred to those comments, not the fact that Bollea was recorded having sex. ...

As reflected in the documents Bollea ultimately produced, an attorney from Los Angeles, Keith Davidson, and his anonymous client proposed transferring to Bollea three video recordings of Bollea having sex with Heather Clem in exchange for a payment of $300,000. As part of what Bollea's counsel described as an FBI "sting" operation, in December 2012, Bollea executed an agreement with Davidson, and then Bollea and David Houston (one of Bollea's attorneys in this action) met with Davidson and his "client" at the Sand Pearl Hotel, whereupon FBI agents, who were waiting in an adjacent room, arrested Davidson and his "client." ...

First, Exhibit B to the Davidson Agreement confirms that Bollea was recorded having sexual relations with Heather Clem on three different occasions on three different dates.

Second, Exhibit B to the Davidson Agreement also includes specific dates for two of the three recordings ... July 3, 2007 and July 13, 2007 ... and sufficient identifying information about the July 13, 2007 recording (e.g., that "Bostick"/Bollea declares "I can't believe I just ate—I feel like a pig") to make clear that it is the one from which excerpts were published on Gawker's website.

Third, Exhibit B to the Davidson Agreement also reflects that another of the three recordings includes a statement by Bubba the Love Sponge Clem (identified by the initials "TAC," for "Todd Alan Clem," his former name) telling Heather Clem that if they wanted to retire they could get rich off the "footage." Significantly, however, Exhibit B indicates that Clem's reference to getting rich from the footage was not about the depiction of Bollea having sex, but instead referred to Bollea's repeated use of racial epithets (comments redacted by Bollea and his counsel). ... ("if we ever did want to retire, all we have to do is use that ... footage of him talking about [REDACTED] people").

Thus, by the time Bollea served his initial responses to Gawker's and Daulerio's discovery requests in August 2013, and, in most cases, by the time this action was amended on December 28, 2012 to include claims against Gawker and the other Gawker Defendants, Bollea and his counsel knew:

That there were at least three recordings depicting Bollea and Heather Clem having sexual relations on three separate occasions.

That two of those recordings had precise dates on them in July 2007.

That two of the recordings were labeled "Hootie," a nickname bestowed on Bollea by Bubba Clem.

(...)

That the Government had retained possession of the three video recordings of Bollea having sexual relations with Heather Clem specifically in connection with this case.

Bollea and/or his counsel also made numerous misrepresentations about the date on which the video excerpted by Gawker was recorded, even though they have known since at least November 2012 that it was recorded on July 13, 2007, knew the date of a second encounter, and knew that the third date was within a matter of weeks of the other two, as Bollea testified under oath at his deposition...whether he had previously discussed his sex life and the size of his penis on Clem's radio program at the time the recordings were made; and whether he had heard about Clem's recording equipment, including in radio broadcasts in which Clem discussed his surveillance system, by the time the recording was made.

In sum, having concealed and then withheld documents that would demonstrate that Bollea was personally involved in the FBI investigation, including the sting operation itself, Bollea and his counsel orchestrated his testimony so that he alternately asserted privilege over....

Finally, during his deposition, Bollea denied having seen any documents and then denied knowing anything about, the entire Davidson affair, including the agreement that he signed personally and the meetings he attended personally....

Bollea and his counsel have justified these redactions on

the basis that Judge Case sustained an objection during the deposition of Bubba Clem to two questions asking generally about Bollea's use of "the 'N' word." ... ("have you ever heard the Hulk use the 'N' word when talking about African-Americans?" and, after pointing to a story on www.thedirty.com that reported on a sex tape involving Bollea including what he "said about black people," asking "Having seen that, do you recall whether Hulk Hogan ever used the 'N' word?").

Even now, and even in court papers filed under seal, Bollea and his counsel are taking a similar approach of denial. On the one hand, the Confidential Affidavit of Charles J. Harder ... as well as Bollea's separate Motion for a Protective Order ... all confirm that the various redacted language is "race-related." On the other hand, they argue that there is "no competent, authenticated evidence of Plaintiff ever having used offensive language of this type."

(...)

Confidential List of Persons Known to Have Possessed, Viewed and/or Had Access to the Video and/or Audio with the Racist Language

- Bubba the Love Sponge Clem;
- Heather Clem;
- Terry Bollea and David Houston, who viewed the relevant portions of the tape with the racist language during a December 2012 meeting with Keith Davidson, the alleged extortionist...
- Keith Davidson;
- Vilma Duarte, Davidson's paralegal who worked

with him on the attempted sale of the tapes to
Bollea...;
- Davidson's unidentified client;
- Lori Burbridge, a woman who accompanied
  Davidson to the December meeting, but whom we
  understand not to have been Davidson's actual
  client...showing L. Burbridge as a signatory...(email
  from D. Houston to FBI agent, indicating that the
  "young lady present during the course of
  negotiations with Davidson admitted that she was
  only an intermediary" for Davidson's client);
- A woman whose name is redacted in the documents
  produced by the FBI, and who is described in those
  documents as having "watch[ed] all three tapes" and
  having "confirmed that BOLLEA used the 'N-word'
  during one of the tapes...
- An unidentified person who, in March 2012, sent a
  "timeline" of two of the sex tapes, including the one
  in which the racist language occurs, to Richard
  Peirce, a former employee of the Bubba the Love
  Sponge Show...who then circulated the timeline to
  others in the Tampa and New York radio
  communities;
- Nik Richie, publisher of TheDirty.com;
- Whoever provided a copy of the tape with the racist
  language to Nik Richie;
- Multiple persons at TMZ, including Mike Walters;
- Whoever provided a copy of the tape with the racist
  language to TMZ;
- Whoever was a source for the *Philadelphia Daily*

*News* article about the racist language on the tape that was published in October 2012;

- Whoever was a source for the Daily Beast article about the racist language on the tape that was published in October 2012;
- Whoever was a source for the Hollyscoop article about the racist language on the tape that was published in October 2012;
- Multiple persons at the FBI, including FBI employees in the Tampa field office who investigated the alleged extortion and FBI employees in Florida and Winchester, Virginia who have worked on the response to Gawker's FOIA request;
- Multiple persons at the Office of the U.S. Attorney, including employees of the Office of the U.S. Attorney for the Middle District of Florida who investigated the alleged extortion and employees of the Executive Office of the United States Attorneys who have worked on the response to Gawker's FOIA request;
- Multiple persons at the Tampa Police Department, which requested and received from the FBI copies of the tapes…(documents provided by the FBI indicating a detective with the Tampa Police Department "viewed all three disks," and that copies of them were later provided to the Tampa Police Department "based on their request for these items as they pertain to an ongoing criminal investigation");
- Multiple persons at the Hillsborough County State's

Attorney's Office, which worked in tandem with the Tampa Police Department on the investigation described in the immediately preceding bullet point; and

- Personnel of this Court and the federal court.

# 5

## Both Sides Argue Before The Judge

**Court hearing before The Honorable James R. Case, July 18, 2-14 regarding access to information about alleged racial comments not admissible before:**

### GAWKER ATTORNEY SETH BERLIN:

Your Honor, when the issue of the N word came up—and this was at Mr. Clem's deposition first—the plaintiff and his counsel, once again, concealed knowledge of multiple tapes, saying, you know, there was only one tape from which the excerpts were made, and that that tape doesn't have any of the language on it, so we shouldn't be able to ask the questions, even though at the time they would have known that there were, you know, transcript—there was a transcript of two other tapes, which included this language, and explains that Mr. Clem's pivotal, We can get rich off of this comment, was on its face, not about the fact that Mr. Bollea had had an affair with Ms. Clem and sex depicted on this tape, but was about his use of racist language on the tape.

And that testimony—I'm sorry, that information, had we been able to get it and get at it, would have substantially undercut Mr. Clem's testimony and the plaintiff's testimony about what a great role model he is and what a great father he is, while he's depicted on this tape using racist language to talk about his daughter and her boyfriend....

And what we learned was that there were at least three recordings depicting Mr. Bollea and Ms. Clem having sexual relations on three separate instances. We learned that two of those recordings have precise dates on them of July of 2007. Two of the recordings were labeled Hootie, a nickname bestowed on Mr. Bollea by Mr. Clem; that on one of the recordings Mr. Clem tells his wife that they could, quote, unquote, retire off the tape, not because it depicts Mr. Bollea having sex, but because it depicts him repeatedly using racist language about black people, including specific people; that Bollea had personally participated in the FBI investigation, including a meeting directly with Davidson, his client representative; that the FBI declined prosecution; and that the government had actually retained possession of the three video recordings of Bollea having sexual relations with Ms. Clem, specifically in connection with this case.

And I would say, Your Honor, that taken together, that series of facts that we learn now—I mean, I look back at all of the work that our whole team has done trying to unravel factually what happened here and think to myself, If I had known this back in October or November when Judge Campbell ordered it, we would have saved—I can't tell you how much—energy and effort trying to prepare this case and move it forward....

So, for example, when the plaintiff says which is a tale that he's told publicly many times—that, you know, in a moment of weakness, he gave in to Mr. Clem and Mrs. Clem and had sex with Mrs. Clem. And, in fact, we now know that that happened four times. It makes it a little less believable that it was sort of in just one moment of weakness.

So what we're asking for is sort of what I'd like to describe as a reverse preclusion order, which is to say instead of saying that the facts would be artificially truncated, that, instead, Mr. Bollea would be precluded from arguing that the things that he concealed did not happen....

So this is—so the things that we're talking about that we would be, you know, that precluded from arguing against is that there were four encounters, that the FBI has three tapes, that there was an alleged extortion attempt and an FBI sting operation, which is obviously about whether this is newsworthy and who gave this tape to Gawker and so forth. And that's because we don't think that the plaintiff should be rewarded for having concealed that information for a year and then misrepresented it to you and to Judge Campbell. And that seems like the proper kind of preclusion order.

And for what it's worth, Your Honor, Gawker, for whatever everyone thinks about it, is really—it's about—it's about the truth. And so, you know, part of this is consistent with what Gawker is about, which is to say, Look, the truth is sometimes embarrassing, sometimes it's uncomfortable, sometimes it's unpleasant. But if we're going to have a trial, we shouldn't have a trial where the version of what's going on is some artificially truncated story. And so that is, I think, a key piece of this....

**HULK HOGAN'S LAWYER CHARLES HARDER:**

We've produced over 2,000 pages of documents in this case, so redacting out five words—and these are words, Your Honor, they are racial words, and Your Honor had previously ruled that they were off limits in the case.

But the point is that we did not conceal that. They had never asked for those documents before. One of the documents that they've presented in their motion was, if I have it here, tapes. Mr. Bollea has never seen any of those tapes. Nobody on either side of this table or Your Honor or Judge Campbell has ever seen any of these supposed tapes. We don't know if they exist or not. Nobody has seen them. Maybe they exist and maybe they don't.

An extortionist said they exist, an extortionist who wanted money and wanted to make certain representations of what was in the supposed tapes, that there is racial comments, that there is all kinds of other comments in there, nobody has seen any of these things.

But yet Mr. Berlin says these tapes exist. He told you that about ten times. These tapes exist, and I concealed that. Nobody has seen them. I haven't concealed anything. I don't know if they exist. When he asked for communications with the FBI, we produced it.

Those communications had in their communications from an extortionist saying, These are the—these tapes exist, and these are what's on them. We produced them. They have it....

We asked for documents about their internal communications regarding the sex tape, the sex tape that they posted. Notice that everything they talked about had nothing to do with their sex tape; it's other tapes that may or may not exist. It's so far afield what they're talking about.

But we asked for the communications in discovery, their internal communications and external communications regarding the actual sex tape.

They withheld that from us for eight months. We took their deposition.

Yes, 32 pages of the 1Ms between all of your employees making fun of Hulk Hogan. They withheld that from us for eight months. And it was not—we didn't even—and they concealed it from us, if you want to use that term that Mr. Berlin loves to use, because they never told us about those things until we were taking depositions, and their employees said that they had internal communications. And they had a specific term for it.

They eventually produced those communications. It was a lot. And it was embarrassing stuff. It was their employees making fun of Hulk Hogan in this actual sex tape that they posted up to the Internet. Did we file a motion for sanctions over that? No, we did not. ...

They received an anonymous DVD that was 30 minutes long of Mr. Bollea having sex with somebody in a private bedroom. And it was not something that they had created, like a private sex tape. This was something where—and you heard Mr. Clem testify. It was like that little motion detector that's way up in the corner of the room that's painted the same color as the wall. It was a surreptitious tape. It was a hidden tape, a hidden camera.

They received a copy of it. They didn't make any inquiries with Mr. Bollea about whether he approved this, whether this was something that he wanted to be out there. They simply immediately edited it down into, in the words of their own editor-in-chief, a highlight reel. That's the words of their editor-in-chief. They created a highlight reel, a minute and 41 seconds of the greatest sexual events that happened on that 30-minute tape. That's what they posted up to the Internet....

One of the sanctions that they asked for in their papers, but Mr. Berlin did not mention—and maybe he mentioned it kind of in a roundabout way—they want to be able to call Mr. Bollea a racist to the jury. They want to be able to parade around the "N" word to the jury. Just so it's clear, there is no competent evidence that he ever said the "N" word. All we have is an extortionist who writes in a document summarizing a tape that may or may not exist saying that in that tape the "N" word is used in some other words that are right around, you know, other racial types of words that are within the same context. …

It's inappropriate on so many levels for them to be able to parade the "N" word and other types of words in front of a jury. I mean, what they want is to win the case in a roundabout way. They want to be able to poison the jury of Mr. Bollea.

(…)

But these words that we redacted out, consistent with your prior ruling, don't have to do with our claims. They don't have to do with their defenses. They don't have to do with the video that was posted. And the substantial concern that we have, for anyone who reads and follows the press and sees what happened to Paula Deen when she was asked about the question, Did you ever use the "N" word—it was actually a racial discrimination case where that issue actually was part of the case, and I believe she said yes. And then the next thing you know her entire empire comes crumbling down.

And a more recent example is Don Sterling, where she tapes him saying something that's racially insensitive and posts it to the Internet, and then he loses his right to be in basketball ever again and has to pay $2,000,000 in sanctions and has to divest himself of everything that has to do with basketball.

As we presented at the Bubba Clem deposition, the stakes are very high on an issue like this. And just to clarify, we're not admitting that this word or these few words were ever uttered by Mr. Bollea. These things show up on an extortionist's summary of alleged tapes that are not even at issue.

But because the stakes are so high, we have to protect our client from a situation like this that we have seen happen to others. And particularly given that these words are not relevant to the case, not reasonably calculated to lead to admissible evidence, we think it was appropriate that we redacted out these words. And we think it's appropriate that Your Honor made the ruling that you did at Bubba Clem's deposition.

We don't think that if these words are disclosed to Gawker that they are going to lead to anything that's admissible in the case. We are not trying to prevent Gawker from getting anything that's relevant in the case....

So it is a realistic concern that we have, that a defendant that is so aggressive in their defense of this case, where in our view they are doing everything in their power to stop this case from going to trial, to stop Mr. Bollea from having his day in court, where their own record is that they have very little regard, if not zero regard, for people's privacy.

I think I put in other papers in the past that the CEO,

Nick Denton, was interviewed by *Playboy*. And a question was asked of him, Is it true that Gawker gives lesser regard of privacy to people?

And his answer was, I don't think people give a fuck about privacy. ... I guess we're now into the issue of the racial, and he was talking about the Daulerio e-mails. And I think it was basically the connection of Tony Burton, agent of the Buchwald agency to all this. He said there two separate individuals who they believe created the summaries. We looked at these summaries, and it looked like it was the same person who created them, and they may have tinkered with them.

But in any event, whether it's one person or two people, it's irrelevant to the fact that racial language was never in their possession of their video. They never published it. They never published a narrative about it. It's not part of their story. It's not part of their claims. It's not part of their defenses to us. They want to find out all things related to the sex tape. Are there more than one tape? Even though it's far afield, they're conducting that discovery, and that's fine. They have received these summaries here.

Where did I put those, from the extortionist? They have it. They have all the information that they need in order to conduct their discovery into the extortion issue.

The fact that we took out five words—I'm happy, again, Your Honor, if you feel it's necessary, I'm happy to show you an unredacted version with highlighting—

**JUDGE JAMES R. CASE:**
That's okay. ... All right. I have had the opportunity to

review all the materials that have been furnished to me prior to the hearing here today. I have also had the opportunity to listen carefully to the arguments which have been propounded to me, and on both sides you have represented your clients very capably. And I have thoroughly enjoyed hearing these arguments. I know you get to make them, but I get to hear them. And after all those years on the bench, I used to dread these kinds of hearings, because most of the time the lawyers are not as competent you are, and you do a good job, so I appreciate that.

But in the final analysis, any analysis with respect to sanctions in the Florida courts are still governed by the case of *Kozel v. Ostendorf,* which is an old Supreme Court decision which is still good and still followed....

And applying that analysis, I come to the conclusion that the defendants' motion is—will be denied in its entirety. I will take advantage of Mr. Harder's offer to have Mr. Bollea submit for limited issues on another deposition with respect to the matters that may have been raised by the release of the FBI records. But other than that, I think that's about as far as it ought to go.

# 6

# Bubba The Love Sponge Testifies

**Highlights from depositions of Todd Alan Clem (AKA "Bubba the Love Sponge") recorded on March 3-4, 2014:**

Q. Hulk told Howard Stern that having sex with Heather was one of the worst decisions he had ever made in his life. Did he tell you that?

A. No. But it was. It's very truthful. It's—it's—that's very dead on.

Q. Prior to the tape coming out, did he ever say anything like that to you?

A. I think he struggled with it.

Q. What did he say?

A. I don't know. We didn't have that conversation.

Q. Why do you think he struggled with it?

A. I don't—I just in my opinion, I think that he struggled with it. I think he was—I think he was in a bad time, and—and I preyed upon his vulnerability, and I—I think it was a bad time for Terry.

Q. What do you mean by that?

A. I think he was going through a tough divorce, and he was just in a bad place, and I think I preyed upon his vulnerability....[Terry Bollea] is a very private dad who—whose family means very much—a lot to him and who doesn't necessarily enjoy drama or—or any type of fame other than just to do his best.

Q. Well, how—how is that different than the Hulk Hogan character?

A. Well, when Mr.—Mr. Hogan is in the four corners of a wrestling ring, there is a time to be Hulk Hogan and there is a time to be Terry Bollea. His closest friends, his ex-wife, probably his current wife, call him Terry. They don't call him Hulk. They call him Terry. He's Terry. When he's not wrestling, he's Terry. He doesn't—if he was full of himself and he wanted to be Hulk Hogan, he would tell you to make sure you call me Hogan or Hulk. I never saw that. People that knew him as Terry called him Terry. And that's how—that's how you could differentiate or how people could differentiate whether he's—the camera is on or off, per se, with regards to working for the wrestling industry or the entertainment business.

Q. And what did you call him?

A. Both. Terry and Hulk, I mean—or Hogan or Hootie. His nickname was Hootie to me, just kind of a term of endearment, Hootie, kind of a play on words.

Q. And how did that come about?

A. Oh, just—just—just Hootie was Hootie. That's just how—it just kind of came.

Q. Did anybody else call him that?

A. Well, people in the show and stuff would call him Hootie.

Q. How did you decide when to call him Terry and when to call him Hulk or Hogan or Hootie?

A. There was no rhyme or reason as to how. I mean, there is

no rhyme or reason. I didn't specifically call him Terry when he was at home or Hogan when he was wrestling. It was just whatever—I very rarely called him Hulk. It was pretty much Terry or Hootie. I can't think of hardly any times that I ever called him Hulk.

Q. What was he known for when you-all were close friends?

A. Well, in my opinion, he's—he's noted as being one of the, you know, most famous people in the—in the world who got famous through—he was pretty much right there at the—when wrestling went from a Pay-per-View, watch-it-in-theaters type deal, into your living room, Terry was very instrumental in that progression. And, you know, obviously, the *Rocky III* movie propelled him into that arena as well...

Q. When was the first time that Heather and Hulk had sex?

A. Well, the first and only time was that time that you guys have the videotape of.

Q. Do you recall what year that was?...

A. No.

Q. And had they had any sexual contact before?

A. No, not—not—I don't think so.

Q. And so if I understand the chronology, you mentioned this to Hulk, and then at some point—at some point shortly thereafter, they had sex?

A. Yes.

Q. And as far as you know, they only had sex one time?

A. Yes.

Q. Do you know, just roughly, what year this was?

A. No.

Q. Do you know whether they ever had any sexual encounter at the radio station where you worked?

A. Yes.

Q. And at that point, this wasn't affecting your friendship, then, over that summer?

A. Not that—not that I can recall. He—he believed me.

Q. Do you recall ever joking around with [Hogan] about [having sex with your wife]?

A. No. This is not a joking matter at all.

Q. Okay. Did you ever recall joking around with him about having sex with Heather during that time period?

A. Well, obviously, we've had some parody elements here.

Q. During this time period.

A. I can't recall what we joked around about. I would probably say no.

Q. Going back to the—well, have you ever heard the Hulk use the "N" word when talking about African-Americans?

MR. HARDER [lawyer for Hogan]: I will object.

(...)

I think that's outside the scope, Your Honor. I don't think this has anything to do with this case, which is about Gawker posting a sex tape. And I think it's in the wake of what's happened in the Paula Deen [case] recently, with the leak of one time using the "N" word inappropriately, albeit in a confidential communication with her husband, and seeing what that did to her career, I just think that this needs to be treaded around very lightly, especially when this is not a quote from either Mr. Hogan, nor from Mr. Clem.

(...)

It's an anonymous quote. I don't think it's fair game....Your Honor, on the Paula Deen issue, that was in a videotaped deposition. That's where it ended up coming out and became an issue at trial when it ended up costing her dearly financially. So what we're trying to do is prevent Gawker from doing the same thing that happened to Paula Deen when there is zero relevance to that in this case...

MR. BERLIN [lawyer for Gawker]: Your Honor...One of the issues that Mr. Harder omitted from his list of issues that are at issue in this case is whether what's on this tape, and if there are other tapes, is newsworthy. We've had a whole bunch of litigation about that. That's been up to the court of appeals, which has ruled on this subject. The question that's being asked is, obviously, something that would go to whether it's being newsworthy....But to be able to get to what's actually going on here, including the motivations for various people about disseminating or not disseminating what's on this tape is key. And that, coupled with somebody who would be a celebrity making what would obviously be newsworthy comments, is something that we need to be able to explore. And it's not something that we're just making up. It's something that's based on published reports that Clem—that were already in the public discussion long before Gawker came on the scene.

THE COURT: If you don't know, then we don't know.

MR. BERLIN [lawyer for Gawker]: One of the questions...that's why we're asking the question. If there is nothing there, then let the witness answer the question.

(...)

MR. BERRY [lawyer for Gawker]: And, Judge Case, if I may just interject. These images on The Dirty are not the images that are on the full DVD.

THE COURT: Okay. Objection sustained.

MR. HARDER: Thank you…

MR. BERRY: Before the break, we were talking about the time period following the April Internet reports on The Dirty and on TMZ. You talked a little bit about the summer period. I'd like to fast-forward now, if we could, to the October 2012, when Gawker posted the—its story and the excerpts from the sex tape. How did you find out that Gawker had published those excerpts?

MR. HARDER: Your Honor, about the content of the tape. There is two tapes. One is the minute 40 seconds that Gawker posted on the Internet. There is nothing about anything racial at all in that. And they produced to us a 30-minute video. There is nothing racial that has to do with that. What we're talking about here is thedirty.com, which is making some sort of an allegation about the content of the tape, that I assume that they are talking about the tape that they provided to us that doesn't have any of this. So now it's become this—this attempt to try to find something to pin on him that's outside of the scope of the case, has nothing to do with newsworthiness, because if they are claiming that something in that tape is newsworthy, they never put it up on their website and they never produced it to us. So this is something that's outside of that scope.

MR. BERLIN [lawyer for Gawker]: We—we don't know what's on the full tape. We know what's on the tape that was provided to us, which is not necessarily the full tape. And we're trying to get to the bottom of this.

A. Well, I—I was told to look, so I went to gawker.com and looked at them.

Q. Who told you?

A. Probably my guy, Brent. Probably Brent or—probably Brent.

Q. Do you recall specifically that conversation?

A. No.

Q. And after that person told you, what's the next thing that you did?

A. Oh, I don't know other than I was probably frantic, you know, freaked out. I'm just speculating. I don't remember that specific day. It wasn't a very good day for me.

Q. Did you go—this is from that person telling you—did you go straight to a computer to look at it?

A. Again, I start preparing for my show at 4:45 in the morning. I don't know if it was the night before that it—I don't know the chain of events subsequently on how—when and how and by what means I looked at it, whether it was my iPad or where. But, you know, I get to the station at 4:45 a.m. We go on at 6:00. I don't know if it was during that preparatory period or not that I saw it…

(…)

Q. When was the first time that Heather and Hulk had sex?

A. Well, the first and only time was that time that you guys have the videotape of.

Q. Do you recall what year that was?

A. No.

Q. And had they had any sexual contact before—

A. No, not—not—I don't think so.

Q. And so if I understand the chronology, you mentioned this to Hulk, and then at some point—at some point shortly thereafter, they had sex?

A. Yes.

Q. And as far as you know, they only had sex once?

A. Yes.

Q. Do you know, just roughly, what year this was?

A. No.

Q. Do you know whether they ever had any sexual encounters at the radio station where you worked?

A. I think so, yeah.

Q. There was nothing awkward about it?

A. Uh-uh (indicates negatively). I knew in the back of my mind that I had wronged him.

Q. But just relate—you mean as far as the recording?

A. Yes.

Q. So you had—when was the—did you realize that you had recorded him?

A. Well, I knew, obviously, when it happened. I knew—I knew that I had surveillance.

Q. Okay. Before the existence of that tape was reported, did you discuss the fact that Hulk and Heather had had sex with anybody else?

A. I don't think so.

Q. Do you know if she did?

A. I can't speculate as to what she did. I don't think she did.

Q. Do you know if Hulk did?

A. I can't speculate, but I would assume no.

Q. But as far as you know, he didn't?

A. I would assume no.

(...)

Q. In the realm of sensitive things that you talked about—again, I'm not asking you to give me any specifics. In what kind of areas would you share sensitive things?

A. All areas, financial, romantically, business, kids, the weather, his father's health. It was a plethora. You know, there is nothing that was out of bounds with regards to a topic that we could possibly speak about.

Q. Did you talk to him about your sex life with Heather?

A. Occasionally, yeah.

Q. Again—

A. But then if I may preface, I spoke on the air about my sex life with Heather. So, I mean, you have to understand that Mr. Bollea wasn't necessarily privy to some kind of inside stuff. I'm—my show is very open, and so it wasn't necessarily, you know, privileged per se.

Q. Were there things that you told Mr. Hogan about your sex life with Heather that were not things you shared on the air?

A. I can't recall specifically. I didn't control my own destiny, other than doing a very stupid thing unbeknownst to him. So it's horrible. It's horrible. And I would like—I apologize now and for the rest of my life will be sorry for what I did.

Q. And what did you do?

A. I—I had videotape of him against his knowledge.

Q. Okay. How would you describe Hulk Hogan now?

A. I'm assuming he hasn't varied from when I knew him. He's just, you know, probably a little bit more cautious. If I was him, I would feel very double-crossed. I'd be very cautious. I would very—I'd probably be very much closed because of, you know, his best friend did him—did him wrong. And I would say that he has a ton amount—a ton of trust issues right now. I don't blame him.

Q. Before when you said that you had videotape of him, did you do the videotaping?

A. I—well, yeah, I did. My—my surveillance system did, but I—you know, it's my system, so—yes, I did.

Q. And you knew you had that videotape?

A. I knew of the system, yes.

Q. But specifically the videotape that you're mentioning, you knew you had videotape of Hulk Hogan having sex?

A. Yes.

Q. Would you describe Hulk as honest?

A. Very.

Q. Trustworthy?

A. Very.

Q. Kind?

A. Very, very.

Q. Do you think he is empathetic?

A. Yes.

Q. Do you think he is compassionate?

A. Very.

Q. Do you think he cares about other people?

A. Yes, to a—to a detriment. I think that Terry—Terry's caring-ness has caused him a lot of pain. I think that he gives way too much and—and people have taken advantage of him a lot.

Q. Have you ever taken advantage of him?

A. Yes and no. I think this situation certainly could be construed as that. Prior to this, no.

(…)

Q. Was he reluctant to have sex with Heather?

A. I think so.

Q. What did he say?

A. Again, I don't recall the specifics of our conversation, but, you know, Terry is very cautious, as he should be, and his caution was correct.

Q. Had Heather pursued Hulk?

A. She always thought that Terry was—was a nice guy and attractive.

Q. Did she pursue him sexually before you had this conversation?

A. I think she might have been flirty—flirty I with him, but I don't know necessarily pursued him sexually.

Q. But nothing in front of you that she made a pass at him?

A. I mean, you know, she was always very nice and cordial to Terry, and so, I mean, you know, I wouldn't say a pass. I wouldn't say that...

(...)

Q. Why—when you—when you mentioned the idea to Hulk about him having sex with Heather, you knew it was going to be recorded?

A. I don't know if I—if I knew at that time or not or it just was a spontaneous-type thing. I don't—I can't give you my mindset as to if I had that mindset or not.

Q. Prior to them having sex, did you know that it was going to be recorded?

A. No. Again, my testimony is I didn't have that mindset per se at the time. It was a spontaneous thing. And again, my room is under surveillance at all times, so I had a certain amount of days, however long my hard drive, whether it was 14 days or 18 days, to captivate that and to save that particular thing. So my testimony would be, no, it was not premeditated at I the time that I asked him. I—I would never do that.

Q. Did Heather understand at that time that she was being

filmed?…

A. I don't know. …

Q. Did you think that she knew she was being recorded?

A. I would assume that she did. I would say the only person who didn't know would be Terry.

# 7

# Heather Cole Testifies

**Highlights from deposition of Heather Cole (formerly Heather Clem) recorded on January 26, 2015:**

Q. Do you recall how many occasions Bubba discussed with you this issue of you having sexual relations with Terry Bollea?

A. I do not recall.

Q. ...Can you give me an estimate? Was it more than five times?

A. I would estimate five or less.

Q. You eventually had sexual relations with Mr. Bollea?

A. Yes.

Q. Do you recall the number of the encounters that you had with him?

A. To the best of my knowledge, I can think of three times that I remember.

Q. Do you recall where those sexual encounters were?

A. Yes.

Q. And where?

A. Once at my—at our house when I was married to Mr. Clem; once at Mr. Bollea's house; once in a hotel room.

Q. Which hotel?

A. I don't recall the name.

Q. Was it located in the Tampa Bay area?

A. No.

Q. Where was it located?

A. Tennessee.

Q. Which happened first? Was it the house that happened first? … Was it—was the first encounter that you had with Mr. Bollea at your house?

A. No. …

Q. Prior to the third sexual encounter, do you recall any communications that you had with either Mr. Clem or with anyone else regarding having sex with Terry Bollea a third time?

A. No, I do not recall.

Q. What do you recall about the third sexual encounter that you had with Terry Bollea?

A. That we had sex.

Q. Do you recall anything else during the time that you had sex—well, strike that. Other than the fact that you had sex, do you recall anything else about the third sexual encounter with Terry Bollea?

A. No.

Q. Do you recall any communications that you had with Bubba Clem or Terry Bollea or anyone else after the third sexual encounter regarding the third sexual encounter?

A. Yes.

Q. What do you recall?

A. At some point after the encounter at our house with Mr. Bollea, Mr. Clem showed me a videotape of myself and Mr. Bollea having sex.

Q. How long did you watch that footage? Was it a few seconds or a few minutes or the whole thing?

A. I did not watch it. It was brief.

Q. What was your response to Mr. Clem when he showed you that?

A. I was upset.

Q. Do you recall what you said to Mr. Clem or what Mr. Clem said to you?

A. I recall being upset.

Q. Did you shout?

A. I don't recall.

Q. I assume that you had no idea before the third sexual encounter that it was going to be filmed?

A. Can you ask me that in a question?

Q. Sure. Did you have any idea before the sexual encounter happened that it was going to be filmed?

A. No.

Q. The first time that you learned of the filming of any sexual encounter with Terry Bollea was after the third encounter, correct?

A. Yes.

Q. Did you ever have any communications with Terry Bollea regarding sex after the third sexual encounter?

A. Not that I recall....

Q. What do you recall of your conversation with Mr. Clem immediately after the third encounter regarding how it was filmed?

A. I don't recall a conversation immediately after the third encounter.

Q. When did the conversation take place that you had with Mr. Clem after the third encounter regarding the filming?

A. I was shown the video. I immediately asked for it to stop. I don't remember a specific conversation. I do remember being very upset.

Q. Do you recall if you asked him to destroy the video?

A. At a later time, yes….

Q. Let me get a sense of the timing. Approximately how much time took place between the third sexual encounter and when you were shown the video of it?

A. I don't recall. …

Q. Do you know whether the camera recorded 24 hours a day?

A. I don't know.

Q. So you don't know whether someone actually needed to actually start and stop the recording?

A. I don't know.

Q. Do you know whether video that was being captured from the camera could be watched while it was recording?

A. I'm not aware.

Q. Do you know whether the video that was captured from that camera was actually being recorded?

A. I don't know.

# 8

# Hulk Hogan Testifies

**Highlights from videotaped depositions of Terry Gene Bollea (AKA "Hulk Hogan") recorded on March 6-7, 2014:**

Q. Did you live with Bubba [radio host Todd Alan Clem, AKA "Bubba the Love Sponge"] at one point?

A. Yes.

Q. For how long?

A. I'm not sure.

Q. Is there some way you would, you know, be able to estimate?

A. Oh, yeah, I could guess. More than a month, definitely not more than two.

Q. Okay. I think that's good. Do you know when that was?

A. Let's see. My wife filed for divorce in November. I just remember I was completely lost after that. And it was sometime after my wife—sometime shortly after my wife filed for divorce, because I was given custody of my beach house. And when I told my divorce lawyer—

MR. HARDER (lawyer for Hogan): Wait.

Hogan: Oh, okay.

MR. BERLIN (for Gawker): Please don't tell me anything you talked to your lawyers about.

A. Okay. I'm sorry. Shortly after I moved into my beach house,

I had to move out because the house was in my ex-wife's name and my ex-wife was trying to put me in jail every week from the gardener said I stared at him, her 18-year-old boyfriend said I stared at him. You know, it was raining, so let's put him in jail....

Q. And did your public image take a hit as a result of the divorce...

A. It was—it really—it really—the public image of Hulk Hogan, the character, basically is Teflon. What took a hit was me on a personal level, because the goodwill of me being able to walk around when I could, walk around without the red and yellow on, and especially in my—especially in my hometown, along with the divorce—my ex-wife said numerous things that weren't true. The numerous things that weren't true, she basically was singing to the heavens that I was a homosexual. And everything was in question such as the homosexual comments. And as much damage as they did, such as a homosexual comment, during the divorce, she just went on a TV show and said, oh, I was just kidding. So with as much I was mad....

Q. And what kinds of things would [Heather and Bubba] say?

A. Well, Heather would get on the phone and tell me, you know, she wanted to see my penis and, you know, just—it just seemed like their ongoing gag to get to me and screw with me....

Q. And did you ever have a conversation with Heather about this in person during that period of time?

A. Not that I can remember.

Q. I'm trying to understand, because you said at the beginning you thought they were serious, but after a while, you thought they may be joking. Did you take what they were saying seriously?

A. Well, you know, Bubba had bragged about him having a swinging lifestyle, you know, where him and Heather had an open marriage, you know. And so when they first approached me, you know, I—I heard on the radio the talk about having parties in the Jacuzzi with friends and buddies and, you know, different doctors and lawyers and people being at his house....At this point, I don't know who all the players are. So it could have been out of loyalty for Bubba. It could be her sexual appetite. It could be some type of perversion for watching tapes. It could be maybe [they] wanted to make money on a tape. Could be all of the above or none of the above. I really don't know the answer to that yet.

Q. What did you think at the time about why she was willing to have sex with you?

A. At the time, I just was under the understanding that it was an open marriage and that was okay with them. ...

Q. Have you watched the full sex tape that was supplied to Gawker and provided to your attorneys in discovery?

A. No.

Q. Do you know whether what's on that tape was the first time or a later time?

A. I've never watched it. So I would have no idea. ...

Q. And when the images appeared on The Dirty, you asked [Bubba Clem] about the tape, right, when you first saw stills or were—

A. No. I didn't see stills on The Dirty. I heard—I heard there were still pictures surfacing. I didn't know if it was dirty or clean or who had them. I just asked him about them.

Q. And when you heard that there were stills, you asked him about the—you asked him about this, right?

A. Yes.

Q. And he lied to you?

A. Yes. He said he didn't know anything about it. He didn't take them.

Q. And you believed him?

A. Yes.

(...)

Q. When you and Bubba discussed you having sex with his wife Heather, did you ask him at that time if he would be filming you?

A. I don't recall asking him that.

Q. Okay. Would you have any reason to ask a question like that? ...

A. He was my friend. I would just answer that again, He would never do something like that.

Q. All right. If you go back to 12:18, the text that appears at 12:18 that we were just looking at, you wrote, I am not waiting for any more surprises because we know there is a lot more coming. Do you see that?

A. I'm sorry. I'm trying to...Where was that at? ...

Q. This is the second line of that text.

A. Yes, I see it.

Q. Okay. I'm not waiting for any more surprises because we know there is a lot more coming. Do you see that?

A. Yes, sir.

Q. Okay. What did you mean by, we know there is a lot more coming?

A. That's privileged.

Q. How so?

A. I heard there was a lot more coming from my attorneys. ...

Q. All right. And when did you learn this?

A. I don't recall. Everything that I learned about there being a sex tape happened after the interview in the hotel room. Because up until then, I saw a couple still pictures and Bubba was lying to me that he didn't do it and Heather did it. So I thought maybe there are just still pictures. So anything about a sex tape happened after TMZ told David and I on the phone that there was a tape going on.

Q. And you're—you're telling us about this interview that occurred on October 9, 2012?

A. Yeah, whatever that date was.

Q. The one when you were in New York?

A. Yes.

Q. Okay. Did you learn anything from someone other than counsel about the number of sex tapes that were out there?

A. I still don't know how many are out there.

Q. Okay. If you would look back at that same text we were looking at, how did you know that one of the tapes had several [REDACTED] slurs?

A. That's privileged.

Q. You learned that from counsel?

A. Yes.

Q. All right. Did you learn information about the [REDACTED] slurs from Mike Walters as well?

A. No.

Q. Did you learn information about [REDACTED] slurs from anyone at TMZ?

A. No, just from counsel....

Q. Looking back at this exhibit here, which was the April 26th publication of The Dirty, it says at the bottom: Terry, do you remember what you said about black people on the sex tape? You are not Dog the Bounty Hunter. Having seen that, do you recall whether Hulk Hogan ever used the "N" word?

MR. HARDER [lawyer for Hogan]: Again, Your Honor, I'm objecting on the same grounds. That has nothing to do with whether Mr. Hogan knew or didn't know that he was being filmed, knew or didn't know about the distribution of the tape, was involved in anything. Those are the subjects of the case. The subject of the case is not a witch hunt about whether he ever used a racial comment or not.

(…)

MR. BERLIN [lawyer for Gawker]: …I'm in the middle of the paragraph where it says—picks up, because I made a bad choice. And the thing that is so disturbing to me is that I have been defending Bubba across the board because I asked him, where did the camera come from? I even asked you, because you know—because I know you have security cameras in your house, you're not filming this, are you? He was like, no, I would never do that to you. How dare you insult me. When the pictures came out, I said what's up? This was on your watch. And he said, oh, it must have been Heather that did it. It's crazy, dude. You've got to stop this….I don't recall saying this. And if I did, you can immediately see I misspoke, because I asked him, where did the cameras come from? And then later on in the article, if I said this, I—I also said, I did not know the cameras were there. So I must have misspoke during the interview. I was so riled.

Q. So for this purpose, it doesn't refresh your recollection of having any conversation with Bubba about there being cameras in his house?

A No. I don't remember this article at all....

Q. During what years was your divorce being litigated?

A. It was being litigated, meaning going to—what years was I going through the divorce?

Q. Yes.

A. She filed in November of '07, and it went on for about three and a half to four years.

Q. And you spoke publicly about that being a low point in your life?

A. Yes.

Q. All right. That says, "Subject to and without waiver of the objections, responding party does not remember the exact number of sexual encounters with Heather Clem. To the best of responding party's recollection, there were at least two and possibly three sexual encounters with Heather Clem in her private bedroom at the Clems' residence and one brief sexual encounter with Heather Clem at the radio station of Todd Clem's radio program. To the best of responding party's recollection, these encounters all occurred in approximately late spring or early summer of 2007, after responding party had separated from his wife." Is this still your recollection about how many times you had sex with Heather?

A. To the best of my recollection, yes.

Q. Did all of the sexual encounters take place in close proximity time-wise to each other?

A. What would you call close proximity?

Q. Well, let me ask you that. How far apart were they?

A. I seem to remember one encounter was four or five days

apart from another one. And then another encounter was like two weeks apart. So it varied.

(…)

Q. And did you have subsequent conversations with either Mr. Clem or Mrs. Clem about that subject [sex with Mrs. Clem]?

A. Yes.

Q. How many such conversations would you say?

A. Over a year-and-a-half period, between—on the phone and between—gosh, I wouldn't even know where to go with this. Between 20 and 40 maybe, maybe more. I don't know. Not more than 40, but between 20 and 40. They kept bringing it up.

Q. Did you ever talk about it with Mr. Clem in person?

A. Yes.

Q. How many times did you talk about it with him in person?

A. I recall a couple times in my gym, he kept telling me that Heather really wanted to have sex with me or Heather really wanted to see me naked. And I just—and it was in a joking way. I just kept telling him, knock it off. It was—you know, it was to the point it was almost like if you were to poke somebody. He just kept poking me. Like it got to the point of I thought they were serious at first, which was a little weird. But then it got to be almost like a joke, you know, like they would tease me all the time….

Q. Do you recall during one of the encounters telling Heather a story about an argument that you got into with some Coast Guard guys at a strip club and how they ended up throwing a lit cigarette in your gas tank?

A. I don't recall telling her that.

Q. Do you recall the incident itself?

A. Yes.

Q. Focusing specifically on the sexual encounter at the radio station, I think you said it was in Bubba's studio?

A. Yes.

Q. And where was that at the time? Bubba's studio?

A. Yeah.

(…)

Q. When did you first learn that someone was shopping a sex tape involving you?

MR. HARDER [lawyer for Hogan]: Lacks foundation. Assumes facts not in evidence.

HOGAN: That's something I can't talk about. It's from one of my attorneys.

MR. BERLIN [lawyer for Gawker]: When was the first time, other than from one of your attorneys, that you learned that someone was shopping a sex tape involving you?

MR. HARDER: Lacks foundation. Assumes facts not in evidence.

HOGAN: After I received the original information, which is confidential, there were I don't know if it was a Twitter or—I don't know if it was TMZ. I'm not—I don't recall completely, but the theme was [porn company] Vivid wanted to do a deal with me, and there was another porno company that said they had an open checkbook for me if I wanted to get in that business.

Q. At the beginning of your answer, you referred to information that was confidential. Is that confidential because it's stuff that you learned from your attorney?

A. Yes, sir.

Q. All right. Did anyone try to sell the sex tape back to you?

A. No one tried to sell it back to me.

Q. Did anybody—did anybody contact you to offer you the sex tape?

A. No…whether it's a rumor or fact, usually the bottom feeders and the vultures usually all group together. So sometimes it's just the sequence of events, because like attracts like. Usually, if there is anything negative or anything positive, those same type of people usually band together to spread the news…there was a sex tape—and when you use the word "told" or "told to me" it's just—it's a rumor, because I don't know if it's true when somebody tells you something. It made me sick. It pretty much put the brakes on everything I was doing, not only emotionally, but business-wise. Everything was book-ended by having to address the subject on a constant basis, 24 hours a day, even to the point of when I would meet someone, whether it be a father or son or a daughter or mother, mentally, as I shook their hand and looked at them and told them it's nice to meet you and thanks for being a fan and I love you too, thanks for being so loyal, no matter what it was, in the back of my mind it just—there was this overriding negative feeling of, If there is a sex tape, have they seen it, and what do they think of me?

(…)

Q. Did you ever talk to Bubba—other than talking to Bubba—that was first set of questions. Other than talking to Bubba, did you ever have any communications with Bubba in other—any other way, e-mail, text, whatever, about any efforts to get law enforcement involved in investigating how this happened?

A. I already told you several times I don't do e-mail.

Q. Fair enough.

A. But I don't recall any talks with him about getting law enforcement involved....

Q. Does it surprise you now that you look at that to see that?

A. No, because sometimes people talk about the divorce. Sometimes people will talk about my son's accident. But we try not to focus on it, because a lot of times people put this horrible picture up of my son's accident. And usually when Elizabeth Rosenthal is involved—and I tried to bring Jules up to speed—I would say no personal questions about the divorce or the fact that my wife was telling everybody I was a homosexual at that time, or my son's accident. And sometimes they will say, We have to touch on it for—to do the interview. There is some rules made that we may just ask about how your son is doing and move on. We may ask about, Do you talk to your ex-wife? and move on. So anything personal like that usually pertained to the problems I had with my wife and my son.

(...)

Q. When did you first learn that Gawker had published an article about a sex tape involving you?

A. I don't recall.

Q. Do you recall if it was shortly after the article was published?

A. Excuse me?

Q. Do you recall if it was shortly after the article was published?

A. I don't recall. And "shortly" means a day, a month? I mean...

Q. I was going to ask you, you know—let me ask you this.

You were on this media tour. Did you learn about the fact that Gawker had published a story about a sex tape involving you before you went on this media tour?

A. Yes.

Q. But you otherwise have no specific recollection of how soon after the article was published you learned about it?

A. It was in close proximity, because the media tour was booked, whether it was booked a week before I went or six months before I went. The media tour was booked, but it seemed like it was closer to the time when I was supposed to go. And I just remember it just being real intense, and I just remember whenever the awareness level grew to an all-time high, it was right before I went on the media tour. So maybe it had been just released then by Gawker, or maybe it was the first time Gawker put it on the website. I just remember the media tour was booked and everything was fine, and all of the sudden, it was like, oh, my gosh, the sex tape is available through Gawker, and should I go or not go on the tour? That was in my mind.

Q. What was your thinking there?

A. My thinking was, I'm not going to hide from anything.

Q. So you decided to go on the media tour even though you had to know people were going to ask about the sex tape?

A. I didn't know if they would ask me or not, but I was going to go and face whatever music I had to face. I wasn't going to hide.

(...)

Q. And did you personally tell any of the producers for these programs when you were arriving that you did not want to talk about the sex tape?

A. Never.

Q. Okay.

A. That's not my job.

Q. Did you consider taking the position that you could not talk about the sex tape because it was going to be the focus of litigation?

A. I don't recall that.

Q. Were you embarrassed to be talking about these things in public?

A. Very embarrassed....

Q. Did you talk about the sex tape at all of the media appearances on the TNA tour?

A. I don't recall.

Q. Do you recall talking about the sex tape on a number of those appearances?

A. Yes.

Q. Were you concerned that by talking about it, you would keep the sex tape story in the news?

A. No. My concern—my concern was—my concern was to stop the rumors and the lies and make people aware, if I could, that we were going to pursue the people that did this to me.

Q. When you say—you refer to rumors and lies. What—what lies are you referring to?

A. Lies that the media would ask me: Is it true that you were knowledgeable that this was being filmed, or is it true that this is just a publicity stunt to get publicity so that you can make millions of dollars on this sex tape? I just wanted to make sure everybody knew that I was not part of anything ever like this....

Q. When you talked to Bubba, did Bubba explain to you how

Heather could have made this film of you…?

A. To the best of my recollection, when I asked him about it, he said Heather must have put a camera up there.

Q. Did you ask—did Bubba explain to you how Heather could have put a camera up there and turned them on without you noticing?

A. No.

Q. After you saw the photographs and Bubba told you that Heather was responsible, did you try and contact Heather?

A. No.

Q. Why not?

A. I have never tried to contact her even when she was friendly to me, so if she had done something this evil or this undermining or this illegal, there would be no reason to contact her.

(…)

(Whereupon, an audio clip [of Clem's radio show] was played as follows:)

MR. CLEM: *All right. How about—how about the people that e-mailed how big is your penis?*

HULK HOGAN: *Man, you guys are brash.*

MR. CLEM: *You guys are brash. You guys are brash. … You tell all your fans right now, you tell all—you keep Brooke at number one on her record release disc, sold Tuesday and all through the week, and I will tell you exactly how big that Loch Ness monster is.*

MR. CLEM: *How big your cock is?*

HULK HOGAN: *Yeah.*

SPEAKER: *Yeah….So that's the fan's motivation?*

MR. CLEM: *Yeah.*

HULK HOGAN: *Well, you tell them.*

MR. CLEM: *Jimmy, we got to keep voting and we've got to buy the—*

HULK HOGAN: *Testify Bubba—testify Bubba, talk smack to your—*

(Audio clip concluded.)

Q. Is that you telling Bubba Clem's listeners that if they help keep your daughter, Brooke's record—or move it to No. 1, you would reveal the size of your penis?

A. It sounds like the Hulk Hogan character talking, yes, in jest, having fun.

(…)

(Whereupon, an audio clip was played as follows:)

HULK HOGAN: *Your cult following.*

MR. CLEM: *Hogan, I—I—I've talked so much smack to them. Look what I've done.*

HULK HOGAN: *Well, if you want to know how big the Loch Ness monster is, you'd better talk some smack.*

MR. CLEM: *I've—I've seen it before. I know how big it is.*

HULK HOGAN: *Shoot, everybody is at (inaudible) has seen it, too.*

MR. CLEM: *Exactly.*

HULK HOGAN: *They call me—they call me King Triton.*

MR. CLEM: *Exactly. I would say hard, you're probably seven and a half or eight inches.*

HULK HOGAN: *Shit.*

MR. CLEM: *That's what I'm saying. I mean, you know, I didn't*

…

HULK HOGAN: *I've got size 15 feet. I wear a size 15 ring on my—wedding ring. Figure it out.*

MR. CLEM: Well, you ain't got a 15-inch cock, Hogan.

HULK HOGAN: No. It's two-thirds the size of your feet and your hands, jack-off.

MR. CLEM: Well, what's 66 percent of 15, Brent?

SPEAKER: Ten.

HULK HOGAN: What the fuck? Where — where — where — what is five times three?

MR. CLEM: So you're saying—Ned said that you're right at 10.

HULK HOGAN: Ned should know. I done bent his ass over enough times. (Laughter.)

SPEAKER: It felt like 10.

MR. CLEM: So Hogan, you're claiming—you're claiming to maybe have a 10-inch cock.

HULK HOGAN: I'm not claiming. Those are the facts, Jack.

MR. CLEM: I wish I was Hulk Hogan with a—

SPEAKER: No way. I'm calling shenanigans.

MR. CLEM: Ten inches?

HULK HOGAN: Huh?

MR. CLEM: Ten inches.

SPEAKER: Now we don't have to vote.

HULK HOGAN: What's that?

MR. CLEM: Nothing. He didn't say nothing, Hogan. All right, Hollywood. Listen—

HULK HOGAN: You guys are all jealous. Ten-inch cock. I really do. I tell you.

(Audio clip concluded.)

Q. Is that you talking about the size of your penis on Bubba Clem's radio show?

A. Now that you've given me more content from that show, it sounds like full-blown comedy, and we were on XM radio, which is uncensored, so we were having fun. And it sounds like nothing but comedy when I talk about bending Ned over, which isn't true, and nothing else on there is true.

Q. But is that you—regardless of whether it's true for a moment, is that you talking about the size of your penis on Bubba Clem's radio show?

A. It's Hulk Hogan talking.

Q. Bubba says: I have seen it before. I know how big it is. When did Bubba see Hulk Hogan's penis?

A. I'm not sure, but he helped me with several surgeries and has been around hospital rooms, and been in my gym when I'm changing clothes. So I'm not sure when he would have looked at me.

Q. And if he did that, he would have been looking at you—he would have been looking at Terry Bollea's penis?

A. I have no idea what he was thinking of when he was—if he—if he was looking, or like I said, just having fun with his comedy routine he's doing.

Q. Were you concerned about your privacy during this broadcast?

A. I don't recall.

# 9

# Summaries Of The Three Hulk Hogan Sex Tapes

**Synopsis of three alleged tape reels containing video footage of individuals taken from a settlement agreement that was part of the court records. To keep identities concealed while negotiating a payout, these reports use pseudonyms and were written by an individual represented by LA attorney Keith Davidson. They are presented exactly as typed.**

*"**Bostick**" is Hulk Hogan*

*"**TAC**" is Bubba "The Love Sponge" Clem, AKA Todd Alan Clem*

*"**F**" is Heather Clem*

*Racial terms are signified by the word "[REDACTED]"*

<u>**Three Reels**</u>

* 1st dated 7-3-07;

* 2nd dated 7-13-07
* 3rd undated
* **FIRST TAPE**
* 43:06 in length
* Residential bedroom—four poster bed
* Starts out with g-string female embracing clothed BOSTICK
* 0:09—TAC enters walks in
* BOSTICK—Good grief, Bubba
* TAC—Isn't she beautiful

1:16—TAC puts music on—female gets on bed wearing only a thong & black pumps. BOSTICK takes his shirt off

* 1:15—TAC walks back in—BOSTICK says wow—this is my Christmas present—TAC responds I'm going to take a shower
* 2:29—BOSTICK standing on floor—female begins performing oral sex on him. Penis is not visible as BOSTICK's back is facing camera. Continues thru 4:48
* 4:48—Hogan turns to camera with erect penis where female continues to perform oral on BOSTICK as he lays on his back. TAC enters—OK I'm going to be in my office watching lookout.

Female responds OK—Continues blowing BOSTICK

* 10:16—BOSTICK breathing heavy Oh Fuck I'm gonna cum oh fuck suck my dick breathing heavy moans, orgasms. Female continues more slowly.
* 11:48—BOSTICK says oh thank you. Female continues…hear kissing sounds as she kisses his penis
* F asks if BOSTICK likes her shoes—yes
* F asks if she can turn shower on for him—yes
* BOSTICK gets up shakes his head & leaves the room.
* 14:30 Female enters wearing nighty & no shoes—gets

dressed gets on bed

BOSTICK reenters naked—F states—all three of us have to go away on a vacation—BOSTICK says no shit … F or else just hang out here for a week

* 15:48—F asks about tension in BOSTICK's family—BOSTICK continues that it was a slap in the face for him to be at a hotel but his family at his house

BOSTICK—there was all these things that added up…it's not like she's leading me on … Thanksgiving only daughter leaves.

* F remains cuddling in bed
* BOSTICK—wife is trying to establish residency in LA …
* 18:15 …I'm just a dumb country bumpkin—my career is over & this is what I have to look forward to
* 19:00—F tells story about trying to park car in a mall—God will reward those who do the right thing
* 20:00—F—you don't have to be anybody's doormat
* BOSTICK getting dressed
* 21:16 F answers phone—
* 22:00 both leave room
* 39:00 F enters—blows out candles—leaves at 40:00
* 43:06 end of tape


* SECOND TAPE 7-13-07
* 30:17 in length
* Same Residential bedroom—four-poster bed
* Starts out with BOSTICK performing oral sex on F
* She is moaning
* TAC says—hey you guys do your thing—I'll be in the office
* 0:38 …F—I want you to fuck the shit out of me today

* BOSTICK I'm so horny—I can't believe I'm here—I should be home
* 1:34—BOSTICK standing—laying on stomach on bed performing oral on BOSTICK while he reaches around fingering her—she is loud
* Sounds of oral sex go thru 4:40 where BOSTICK says, You go…suck my dick
* 5:00 BOSTICK—do you have a rubber
* F opens a drawer gets a rubber but continues giving oral before she puts it on the standing BOSTICK. BOSTICK full frontal—facing camera
* 6:40 BOSTICK slides onto his back in bed she gets on top—intercourse—loud. Kissing.
* 7:28 BOSTICK begins smacking F's ass—she is loud—your big dick is so great—
* 8:21 LOUD F—I'm cumming—fuck yeah—-give it to me
* 8:50 BOSTICK—orgasm
* 9:25—BOSTICK—okaaay—it almost came off. F leaves room
* 10:20—BOSTICK—I can't believe I have to drive back home—
* F returns to a spent BOSTICK—would you like me to turn the shower on for you
* 10:30—BOSTICK I can't believe I just ate—I feel like a pig
* 12:35—naked F reenters—crawls into bed.
* 13:27—BOSTICK reenters—look at you…you are out all cuddly—
* BOSTICK getting my bubba shirt back on crazy … eating like a pig 10 minutes ago
* 14:20 BOSTICK gets dressed … feel like I just got off a

rollercoaster

* 15:00—[Hogan's son] Nick's girlfriend is only 17 she has a killer fucking body.

* The other night Nick is out & the dogs are playing tug of war with Nick's & his girl's underwear ... then Nick has another girl who is even hotter in Orlando—then she wants to be 1st to get me if I'm divorced. ... hot commodity

* 18:30 I got in trouble at OZ—coast guard guys—they give him a bracelet. Buy each other beers. Then they buy a Jagermeister. They challenge BOSTICK to fight. I fight these four motherfuckers.

* They fucked with my car. They put a lit cigarette in my gas tank. Fuck this—I don't care if it is on the front page of the USA today—go back to OZ—get security footage—they piss on car—scratch car—to make a long story short—cab driver interviewed by cops.

* At 4AM police arrest the 4 guys—

* 23:10—...you are awesome—F—so are you

* 30:11—tape ends


* **TAPE 3-UNDATED**
* **50:03 IN LENGTH**
* Residential bedroom—four poster bed
* Starts out with voices of TAC BOSTICK & F talking
* TAC excuses himself
* F talks about off-road biking—nobody in frame
* 2:07 enter F & BOSTICK clothed.
* BOSTICK removes her top
* BOSTICK takes off his TAC shirt

* They get on bed
* 3:06—BOSTICK this is some weird shit. F says I guess so—just roll with it
* 3:56—F turns BOSTICK around he is facing camera and she performs oral as he sits on edge of bed.
* 6:00 BOSTICK lays back in bed as she goes nuts giving oral.
* 6:55 BOSTICK puts condom on
* 7:30 BOSTICK performs oral
* 8:00 BOSTICK intercourse
* F it feels so good
* F—fuck me so good.
* F—oh you are so big—Loud
* F—let me get on top of you
* BOSTICK continues
* 9:15 F—BOSTICK I'm gonna cum loud
* 10:00 F—oh you gotta stop—you are killing me—your dick is so big
* BOSTICK slows down
* 11:00 F leaves—BOSTICK remains on back naked in bed
* 11:50 she returns—washes BOSTICK's penis
* 12:50 the couple cuddles—naked on bed
* 13:30 F—I'm a little worried about you
* 14:00—F you know you can come over here whenever you want & chill out—BOSTICK—I appreciate that
* 17:09—BOSTICK I should probably try to head home & try and beat Nick home. There is so much BS in my life, I want to try & not lose everyone.
* 17:30 I feel bad for Brooke—she is making some real bad decisions now.
* 18:20 F would you like to take a shower? …BOSTICK—That

would be cool—let me rinse off real quick.

* 19:40—both leave room
* 20:34 F returns clothed—goes to nightstand, leaves again
* 21:00 F makes bed—
* 22:00 small talk furniture, etc.
* 22:52—BOSTICK puts Bubba shirt on
* 23:20 BOSTICK MTV called my wife & said they were going to sue her. My wife texted me to say Happy Father's Day because she won't talk on the phone anymore
* 24:00 BLP enters—(the three of them are now in the room). BOSTICK talking about wife's contractual issues with MTV.
* 25:00—BOSTICK Brooke—you better get off your ass & get your mom in gear. I understand having an edge—I know how to work a gimmick.
* 26:22 TAC talking about Linda Hogan—you should go on Oprah, Ellen, etc.
* 27:00—BOSTICK talking about Linda fucking up MTV show
* 27:55—BOSTICK—my daughter Brooke jumped sides on me. I spent 2-3 M on her music. I've done everything like a jackass for her.
* TAC—these fuckers don't realize this old man (BOSTICK) cuts bait…
* 28:40 The one option Brooke had—Brooke's career besides me is South Beach Records—billionaire guy—I don't know if Brooke was fucking the guy's son … whatever …I mean, I know what is going on—I mean I don't have double standards—I mean …to a point. Fucking. But then when it comes to nice people and shit whatever. I mean I'd rather if she was gonna fuck a — I'd rather have her marry an 8 foot tall 100M

basketball player.

* F—We all are a little bit.

* BOSTICK—Cecil—fucking—he had Jamie Foxx coming in on the 22nd track...I didn't even tell Brooke about it. Fuck her.

* 30:54 BOSTICK—Brooke & Cecil meet in Miami—Brooke fucks up a $10M deal I had with the Saudis—Brooke says Fuck You Dad. She's never said that. She flipped a bird at me.

* 32:00 BOSTICK—I have this huge fucking home in Miami. My family never came home. They went to LA :- fuck '

* 34:00—MTV programming—ad buys. Linda fucking quit. And she tried to put it on me.

* 35:00—BOSTICK Brooke was pissed because "I didn't set her up" WTF—thankless.

* 36:00 Linda is fucking nuts. She wants to duplicate our FL house in LA—she is fucking crazy.

* 36:55—Palms place in Vegas—I bought it for 4.25—it is worth 5M. If I get divorced—Linda will make me sell it. But fuck it—Cecil will buy it and give it back to me after the divorce.

* 38:00 BOSTICK—you can think whatever the fuck you want about me but I will never give Brooke the opportunity again to publicly disrespect me b/c I don't trust her.

* 38:50 TAC—BOSTICK I have something for you—your—check it out. (Oakley inscribed glasses).

* 40:10 BOSTICK—dude the only thing I'll ask you & I don't know how you'll pull this off is—if I'm ever on my death bed don't let Linda come & see me.

* 41:00 TAC & Wife then give BOSTICK a thank you card to BOSTICK to give to Linda for the wedding.

* 42:00 BOSTICK ... VH1 wanted me to do a big thing, go

back to the house I grew up in—so we knock on the door & a big [REDACTED] lives there now. The half [REDACTED] was enamored with Linda.

* 43:38 BOSTICK—to F. I love you baby. TAC & BOSTICK leave F in bed.

* 49:00—TAC re-enters & says—if we ever did want to retire, all we have to do is use that fucking footage of him talking about [REDACTED] people.

* 49:45 ... TAC—I want to watch the tape.

* F—his dick hurt so fucking bad—you'll probably just see my face squirming???—I just tried to get past the pain to enjoy it

* 50:03—tape ends

# 10

# Text Messages Between Bubba And Hulk

**Text messages between Bubba Clem and Hulk Hogan,
October 12, 2012, reprinted exactly as typed**

**Bubba:**
Listen u know that i love you terry period. please stop publicly burying me. I didn't release the footage, and im suffering horribly from all this. the thing that hurts the most is that u r upset with Me. I have always tried to protect You /ur family during tragedies far worse than a sex video.

**Bubba:**
Nobody has stood by u more than me….We have so much history. This is a bad deal that was the by product of a very evil woman that I'm very embarrassed to have been married to. I'm very sorry /embarrassed / we both are going thru this. It's not good for me either

**Hulk:**
You told me to tell the truth so how am I burying you, I didn't hear a word from u, u said u were with me and u didn't need to lawyer up then I hear from your lawyer, you did not call me and I got fed to the media lions without another word from

you! I'm losing everything, my job, career and everyone in my personal life and your worried about me burying you by telling the truth? I don't get it and now I finally hear from you and that is how somebody treats their best friend? lie about filming me, say your with me all the way, let me get crucified and now your worried about YOURSELF getting buried by the truth, I just don't get it.

**Hulk:**

I'm a really bad spot and I'm trying really hard to decide who is gonna be in the crosshairs so you need to not bull shit me and answer only one question. Why did you lie to me and tell me there were no cameras filming in your bedroom when you had them set up and ready to film already?

**Bubba:**

Terry. Texting is horrible. Lets sit down next week in person. If u want. Again I'm sorry.

**Hulk:**

We know there's more than one tape out there and a one that has several racial slurs were told, I have a PPV and I am not waiting for anymore surprises because we know there is a lot more coming, all because u filmed me, so I'm asking u one more time, why do u lie to me then film me anyway, I need an answer now because things are moving really fast and I really hope u can make me understand be because I'm not playing anymore games and I'm not waiting for anymore bs lies

**Bubba:**

Terry. Based on the press I've seen you are having a press conference today announcing a law suit against me and Heather. I don't understand why you have chosen to do this at all. I have been there through thick and thin for you over and over again. Now David Houston getting in front of a TV camera is more important than our life long friendship. If you file this suit I will be forced to defend myself and will do so by whatever means are necessary and will disclose EVERYTHING I know about EVERYTHING. I don't want to do any of this but if attacked I will be forced to defend myself and will do so using all means and forums I have available to me. I'd rather work together on this but you do what you need to do and I just want you to be prepared for me to do the same.

**Hulk:**
Your actions speak louder than your words "no words", I asked you to answer one question, no answer, u left me to to be destroyed, my personal life, my career, nothing from u. This isn't about David, it's about u setting me up lying to me and filming me when I had no knowledge of it and all I asked you for was an answer, why did u do this to me but I got nothing from u. Now I understand you we're never my friend and there is nothing more you could ever do to hurt me! Let me guess, tell the truth, I'm not afraid of the truth, maby lie some more, I wouldn't surprised one bit. Now my actions will speak for me. Thanks for never being my friend and destroying my life, "what are friends for?"

# 11

# The Verdict

On March 18, 2016, a six-person Florida jury—four women and two men—decided in favor of Hogan for invasion of privacy. He was awarded roughly $55 million in compensatory damages, $60 million for emotional distress, and $25 million in punitive damages.

Claiming that contradictory statements by Hogan and Bubba Clem—as well as racial comments by Hogan on a separate tape—were unfairly withheld from the jury, Denton and his attorneys promise to appeal the decision.

**Thought Catalog, it's a website.**

www.thoughtcatalog.com

## Social

facebook.com/thoughtcatalog
twitter.com/thoughtcatalog
tumblr.com/thoughtcatalog
instagram.com/thoughtcatalog

## Corporate

www.thought.is